INTRODUCING
ISSUES WITH
OPPOSING
VIEWPOINTS®

Endangered Species

Other books in the Introducing Issues
with Opposing Viewpoints series:

AIDS
Civil Liberties
Cloning
The Death Penalty
Gangs
Gay Marriage
Genetic Engineering
Smoking
Terrorism

INTRODUCING
ISSUES WITH
OPPOSING
VIEWPOINTS®

Endangered Species

Cynthia A. Bily, *Book Editor*

Christine Nasso, *Publisher*
Elizabeth Des Chenes, *Managing Editor*

GREENHAVEN PRESS
An imprint of Thomson Gale, a part of The Thomson Corporation

THOMSON
━━━━✦━━━━ ™
GALE

Detroit • New York • San Francisco • New Haven, Conn. • Waterville, Maine • London

For more information, contact
Greenhaven Press
27500 Drake Rd.
Farmington Hills, MI 48331-3535
Or you can visit our Internet site at http://www.gale.com

LIBRARY OF CONGRESS CATALOGING-IN-PUBLICATION DATA

Endangered species / Cynthia A. Bily, book editor
    p. cm. -- (Introducing issues with opposing viewpoints)
  Includes bibliographical references and index.
  ISBN-13: 978-0-7377-3849-0 (hardcover)
  1. Endangered species--Juvenile literature. 2. Nature conservation--Juvenile literature. I. Bily, Cynthia A.
  QH75.E655 2007
  333.95'22--dc22

                                                    2007031324

ISBN-10: 0-7377-3849-9

Printed in the United States of America

10 9 8 7 6 5 4 3 2 1

Contents

Chapter 3: Are the Needs of Humans More Important than Protecting Endangered Species?

Foreword

Indulging in a wide spectrum of ideas, beliefs, and perspectives is a critical cornerstone of democracy. After all, it is often debates over differences of opinion, such as whether to legalize abortion, how to treat prisoners, or when to enact the death penalty, that shape our society and drive it forward. Such diversity of thought is frequently regarded as the hallmark of a healthy and civilized culture. As the Reverend Clifford Schutjer of the First Congregational Church in Mansfield, Ohio, declared in a 2001 sermon, "Surrounding oneself with only like-minded people, restricting what we listen to or read only to what we find agreeable is irresponsible. Refusing to entertain doubts once we make up our minds is a subtle but deadly form of arrogance." With this advice in mind, Introducing Issues with Opposing Viewpoints books aim to open readers' minds to the critically divergent views that comprise our world's most important debates.

Introducing Issues with Opposing Viewpoints simplifies for students the enormous and often overwhelming mass of material now available via print and electronic media. Collected in every volume is an array of opinions that capture the essence of a particular controversy or topic. Introducing Issues with Opposing Viewpoints books embody the spirit of nineteenth-century journalist Charles A. Dana's axiom: "Fight for your opinions, but do not believe that they contain the whole truth, or the only truth." Absorbing such contrasting opinions teaches students to analyze the strength of an argument and compare it to its opposition. From this process readers can inform and strengthen their own opinions, or be exposed to new information that will change their minds. Introducing Issues with Opposing Viewpoints is a mosaic of different voices. The authors are statesmen, pundits, academics, journalists, corporations, and ordinary people who have felt compelled to share their experiences and ideas in a public forum. Their words have been collected from newspapers, journals, books, speeches, interviews, and the Internet, the fastest growing body of opinionated material in the world.

Introducing Issues with Opposing Viewpoints shares many of the well-known features of its critically acclaimed parent series, Opposing Viewpoints. The articles are presented in a pro/con format, allowing readers to absorb divergent perspectives side by side. Active reading questions preface each viewpoint, requiring the student to approach the material thoughtfully and carefully. Useful charts, graphs, and cartoons supplement each article. A thorough introduction provides readers with crucial background on an issue. An annotated bibliography points the reader toward articles, books, and Web sites that contain additional information on the topic. An appendix of organizations to contact contains a wide variety of charities, nonprofit organizations, political groups, and private enterprises that each hold a position on the issue at hand. Finally, a comprehensive index allows readers to locate content quickly and efficiently.

Introducing Issues with Opposing Viewpoints is also significantly different from Opposing Viewpoints. As the series title implies, its presentation will help introduce students to the concept of opposing viewpoints, and help them learn to use this material to aid in critical writing and debate. The series' four-color, accessible format makes the books attractive and inviting to readers of all levels. In addition, each viewpoint has been carefully edited to maximize a reader's understanding of the content. Short but thorough viewpoints capture the essence of an argument. A substantial, thought-provoking essay question placed at the end of each viewpoint asks the student to further investigate the issues raised in the viewpoint, compare and contrast two authors' arguments, or consider how one might go about forming an opinion on the topic at hand. Each viewpoint contains sidebars that include at-a-glance information and handy statistics. A Facts About section located in the back of the book further supplies students with relevant facts and figures.

Following in the tradition of the Opposing Viewpoints series, Greenhaven Press continues to provide readers with invaluable exposure to the controversial issues that shape our world. As John Stuart Mill once wrote: "The only way in which a human being can make some approach to knowing the whole of a subject is by hearing what can be said about it by persons of every variety of opinion and studying all modes in which it can be looked at by every character of mind. No wise man ever acquired his wisdom in any mode but this." It is to this principle that Introducing Issues with Opposing Viewpoints books are dedicated.

Introduction

We are well into the opening phase of a mass extinction of species. There are about 10 million species on earth. If we carry on as we are, we could lose half of all those 10 million species.

—environmental scientist Norman Myers, 2006

When the United States passed the first Endangered Species Preservation Act in 1966, the issues seemed clear. The whooping crane, one of the rarest and most magnificent birds in North America, was nearly extinct, with fewer than four dozen alive anywhere on the planet. It was clear that the primary reason for the declining numbers was the loss of habitat, and Congress set aside funding for the U.S. Fish and Wildlife Service to buy land to protect the cranes and a short list of other species. In 1969 the protections given to threatened species expanded with a new Endangered Species Conservation Act, this time inspired by a well-publicized international Save the Whales campaign. It seemed obvious to many people that protecting rare and beautiful plants and animals was worth the cost.

For much of the nearly four decades since then, the public's interest in protecting endangered species has been centered on a few species recognized as particularly charismatic: pandas, manatees, wolves, tigers, jaguars, and snow leopards. Environmentalists have welcomed the attention these popular animals have attracted to the issues of protecting endangered species, but they have also noted that it can be difficult to get the public to be concerned about an endangered worm, or moss, or fungus. Explaining the importance of small and less-photogenic species has always been a challenge for the environmental movement.

However, as the twentieth century drew to a close, new and even more difficult challenges became increasingly important for those working to protect endangered species. The first of these growing challenges was global warming. As the earth's temperature increases, fragile habitats are threatened: Alpine plants, as their high-altitude ecosystems become warmer, are being invaded and overcome by trees that normally live elsewhere; penguins and polar bears are declining as the sea ice they normally inhabit in the winter is melting; rising oceans are bringing saltwater into coastal wetlands in Florida; and drought is pushing deserts to overtake plains. One group of scientists predicts that, by the year 2050, as many as 1 million species will become extinct because of global warming. According to conservation ecologist Chris Thomas of the United Kingdom, "climate change now represents at least as great a threat to the number of species surviving on Earth as habitat-destruction and modification."

Another threat to endangered species comes from the world's increasing need for energy. As more parts of the world obtain benefits like electricity and automobiles, and as people in industrialized countries continue to expand their demands for energy, the dangers facing fragile habitats increase. In the United States, where consumption of oil has been steadily on the rise, many people are calling on the federal government to allow drilling for oil in formerly protected areas, including the Alaska National Wildlife Refuge and areas off the coasts, and drilling for natural gas and oil in wilderness areas of the West. Some environmentalists fear that exploration and extraction in these areas will push fragile species out of already shrinking habitats. One answer to the nation's dependence on oil has been an increase in the use of ethanol, often made from corn, but this too carries risks for wildlife. Growing corn relies heavily on the use of chemical fertilizers and pesticides; these chemicals, when washed down the Mississippi River, create a "dead zone" in the Gulf of Mexico, where there is so little oxygen that fish, shrimp, and other marine life cannot survive. In China, an increasing demand for electricity led to the construction of the world's largest hydroelectric dam, the Three Gorges Dam, across the Yangtze River. Several species have found their habitats destroyed, or have become unable to travel to feeding or breeding grounds. The Yangtze River Dolphin was declared extinct in December 2006, largely because of the dam, and other species including the Chinese paddlefish and the Siberian crane have been seriously threatened.

Finally, a new sense of danger from the outside world has led some American citizens to demand that their government place a higher priority on protecting people, even if it means not protecting plants and animals. For example, the U.S. Navy has, since the end of the twentieth century, been developing and improving a new sonar technology that can locate and identify submarines that would have previously gone undetected; however, this sonar technology has been found to occasionally harm whales and other marine mammals. Perceived problems caused by illegal immigration from Mexico have brought about calls for a seven-hundred-mile fence along the United States–Mexico border. Many environmentalists fear that this fence and its floodlights will interfere with the natural migration patterns of the jaguar and the Mexican gray wolf, and cause erosion in fragile habitats. Center for Biological Diversity director Michael Finkelstein believes that the fence will not even stop illegal immigration, claiming that "the only thing it will stop is the biological and cultural diversity that makes the border region so rich and interesting." But, as citizen activists on a We-Need-a-Fence Web site argue, "the first priority of the federal government is national security," and "national security is inherently incomplete if it does not include border security."

Ultimately, it will be governments—acting at the direction of informed citizens—that will determine how to balance the needs of threatened and endangered species against the needs of humans. Those participating in the discussions will need to answer at least three questions: Is extinction a serious problem? Are efforts to help endangered species effective? Are human needs more important than protecting endangered species? These questions are addressed by the authors of the following viewpoints.

Chapter 1

Is Extinction a Serious Problem?

Polar bears were added to the Endangered Species list due to global warming, starvation, and hunters.

Efforts to Protect Endangered Species Are Important

Andrew Buncombe and Severin Carrell

"Climate change threatens the survival of thousands of species—a threat unparalleled since the last ice age, which ended some 10,000 years ago."

In the following viewpoint, Andrew Buncombe and Severin Carrell describe the effects of global warming on the habitat necessary for the survival of polar bears and other species. Because migratory species must travel long distances through changing habitats, they are particularly at risk, according to scientists. Buncombe and Carrell quote scientists who contend that the challenges facing threatened animals are serious and complex.

Buncombe is the Washington correspondent for the London newspaper the *Independent*, and Carrell is the Scotland correspondent for the same paper. They have written extensively about politics and the environment.

AS YOU READ, CONSIDER THE FOLLOWING QUESTIONS:
1. According to Alaska native Charlie Johnson, what caused six polar bears to drown off the coast of Barrow, Alaska?
2. Why has the amount of krill, a primary food of whales and penguins, declined, according to the viewpoint?
3. Why, according to the viewpoint, do some people in the Democratic Republic of the Congo eat gorillas, even though they are endangered?

The polar bear is one of the natural world's most famous predators—the king of the Arctic wastelands. But, like its vast Arctic home, the polar bear is under unprecedented threat. Both are disappearing with alarming speed. Thinning ice and longer summers are destroying the bears' habitat, and as the ice floes shrink, the desperate animals are driven by starvation into human settlements—to be shot. Stranded polar bears are drowning in large numbers as they try to swim hundreds of miles to find increasingly scarce ice floes. Local hunters find their corpses floating on seas once coated in a thick skin of ice.

FAST FACT

As of October 2006, there were 16,119 animals, plants, and lichens on the World Conservation Union's Red List of threatened species around the world.

It is a phenomenon that frightens the native people that live around the Arctic. Many fear their children will never know the polar bear. "The ice is moving further and further north," said Charlie Johnson, 64, an Alaskan Nupiak from Nome, in the state's far west. "In the Bering Sea the ice leaves earlier and earlier. On the north slope, the ice is retreating as far as 300 or 400 miles offshore."

Last year, hunters found half a dozen bears that had drowned about 200 miles north of Barrow, on Alaska's northern coast. "It seems they had tried to swim for shore. . . . A polar bear might be able to swim 100 miles but not 400."

His alarming testimony, given at a conference on global warming and native communities held in the Alaskan capital, Anchorage, last week, is just one story of the many changes happening across the globe. Climate change threatens the survival of thousands of species—a threat unparalleled since the last ice age, which ended some 10,000 years ago.

Scientists Issue Warnings

The vast majority [of species], scientists will warn this week [October 2005], are migratory animals—sperm whales, polar bears, gazelles, garden birds and turtles—whose survival depends on the intricate web of habitats, food supplies and weather conditions which, for some species, can stretch for 6,500 miles. Every link of that chain is slowly but perceptibly altering. . . .

A report being presented [in October 2005] in Aviemore [Scotland] reveals this is a pattern being repeated around the world. In the sub-Arctic tundra, caribou are threatened by "multiple climate change

This map shows twenty "hot spots" where mammals have the greatest risk of extinction.

Mammals in Danger

impacts." Deeper snow at higher latitudes makes it harder for caribou herds to travel. Faster and more regular "freeze-thaw" cycles make it harder to dig out food under thick crusts of ice-covered snow. Wetter and warmer winters are cutting calving success, and increasing insect attacks and disease.

The same holds true for migratory wading birds such as the red knot and the northern seal. The endangered spoon-billed sandpiper, too, faces extinction, the report says. They are of "key concern". It says that species "cannot shift further north as their climates become warmer. They have nowhere left to go. . . . We can see, very clearly, that most migratory species are drifting towards the poles."

The report, passed to *The Independent* [a London newspaper] on Sunday, and commissioned by the [British] Department for the Environment, Food and Rural Affairs (Defra), makes gloomy predictions about the world's animal populations. "The habitats of migratory species most vulnerable to climate change were found to be tundra, cloud forest, sea ice and low-lying coastal areas," it states. "Increased droughts and lowered water tables, particularly in key areas used as 'staging posts' on migration, were also identified as key threats stemming from climate change."

Some of its findings include:

- Four out of five migratory birds listed by the UN [United Nations] face problems ranging from lower water tables to increased droughts, spreading deserts and shifting food supplies in their crucial "fuelling stations" as they migrate.
- One-third of turtle nesting sites in the Caribbean—home to diminishing numbers of green, hawksbill and loggerhead turtles—would be swamped by a sea level rise of 50cm (20ins). This will "drastically" hit their numbers. At the same time, shallow waters used by the endangered Mediterranean monk seal, dolphins, dugongs and manatees will slowly disappear.
- Whales, salmon, cod, penguins and kittiwakes are affected by shifts in distribution and abundance of krill and plankton, which has "declined in places to a hundredth or thousandth of former numbers because of warmer sea-surface temperatures." . . .

Peregrine falcons face harder migrations as a result of polar ice shifts.

Solutions Will Be Complex

The science magazine *Nature* predicted last year [2004] that up to 37 per cent of terrestrial species could become extinct by 2050. And the Defra report presents more problems than solutions. Tackling these crises will be far more complicated than just building more nature reserves—a problem that Jim Knight, the nature conservation minister, acknowledges.

A key issue in sub-Saharan Africa, for instance, is profound poverty. After visiting the Democratic Republic of the Congo last month, Mr. Knight found it difficult to condemn local people eating gorillas, already endangered. "You can't blame an individual who doesn't know how they're going to feed their family every day from harvesting what's around them. That's a real challenge," he said.

And the clash between nature and human need—a critical issue across Africa—is likely to worsen. As its savannah and forests begin shifting south, migratory animals will shift along with them. Some of the continent's major national parks and reserves—such as the Masai-Mara or Serengeti—may also have to move their boundaries if their game species, the elephant and wildebeest, are to be properly protected. This will bring conflict with local communities. . . .

In Alaska last week [October 2005], satellite images released by two US [United States] universities and the space agency NASA [National Aeronautics and Space Administration] revealed that the amount of sea-ice cover over the polar ice cap has fallen for the past four years. "A long-term decline is under way," said Walt Meier of the National Snow and Ice Data Centre.

The Arctic's native communities don't need satellite images to tell them this. John Keogak, 47, an Inuvialuit from Canada's North-West Territories, hunts polar bears, seals, caribou and musk ox. "The polar bear is part of our culture," he said. "They use the ice as a hunting ground for the seals. If there is no ice there is no way the bears will be able to catch the seals." He said the number of bears was decreasing and feared his children might not be able to hunt them. He said: "There is an earlier break-up of ice, a later freeze-up. Now it's more rapid. Something is happening."

And now, said Mr Keogak, there was evidence that polar bears are facing an unusual competitor—the grizzly bear. As the sub-Arctic tundra and wastelands thaw, the grizzly is moving north, colonising areas where they were previously unable to survive. Life for Alaska's polar bears is rapidly becoming very precarious.

EVALUATING THE AUTHORS' ARGUMENTS:

The viewpoint you have just read includes testimony from native Alaskan and Canadian hunters as well as reports from scientists. Why do you think the authors included information from both groups of people? How do eyewitness accounts from "average" citizens contribute to the article?

Efforts to Protect Endangered Species Are Based on False Assumptions

"For at least 10,000 years humans have been the primary forces structuring 'natural' systems, and those systems are in constant change."

Randy T. Simmons

In the following viewpoint, Randy T. Simmons argues that the idea of a "balance of nature" is a myth, a false assumption that leads environmentalists to try to take extraordinary actions to preserve a past that never actually existed. The primary victims of this false assumption, he contends, are landowners, who face restrictions on the uses of their own land in the name of protecting endangered species. He concludes that federal and state governments must work with landowners—not against them—to encourage preservation.

Simmons is a professor of political science at Utah State University and a senior fellow at the Property and Environmental Research Center (PERC), an institute that researches ways to bring market principles to solve environmental problems.

Randy T. Simmons, "Nature Undisturbed: The Myth Behind the Endangered Species Act," *PERC Reports,* March 2005, pp. 3-5. Reproduced by permission.

AS YOU READ, CONSIDER THE FOLLOWING QUESTIONS:
  1. According to wildlife ecologist Charles Kay, where did Meriwether Lewis and William Clark observe the greatest concentrations of wildlife?
  2. Why, according to the viewpoint, were there few wolves in the American West at the time Christopher Columbus discovered the Americas?
  3. Why, according to the viewpoint, are state governments better able to protect species than the federal government?

The Endangered Species Act (ESA) is broken. Indeed, it was born broken. Enacted in 1973, the act is based on the myth of the balance of nature and, in particular, on a flawed understanding of the biological state of the Americas at the time of [Christopher] Columbus's arrival [in 1492]. It is not even an endangered species act; it is an endangered subpopulation and distinct population segment act. And its regulatory approach ignores the role of states and landowners in species protection.

FAST FACT

Scientists estimate that approximately 65 million years ago, a large asteroid collided with Earth and led to the extinction of thousands of plant and animal species, including dinosaurs.

The "balance of nature" is the idea that nature is characterized by constancy and stability. Biologists today understand that there is no balance of nature, there is no ecological stasis, there is only change. Therefore, the Endangered Species Act cannot restore a balance of nature by restoring species. In his book *Discordant Harmonies*, biologist Daniel Botkin observed that the views underlying the environmental laws of the 1970s "represented a resurgence of prescientific myths about nature blended with early-twentieth-century studies that provided short-term and static images of nature undisturbed."

"Nature undisturbed" assumes that the American continents were a wilderness teeming with untold numbers of bison, passenger pigeons,

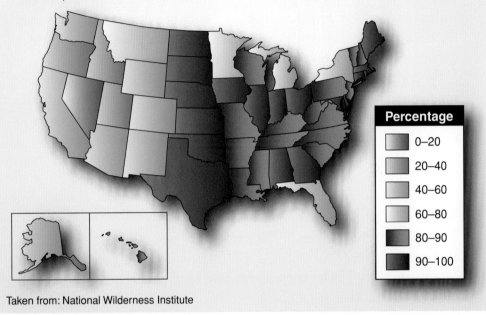

Percentage of Private Land

About 80 percent of threatened and endangered species in the United States have at least part of their habitat on private land. In fact, much of the land in the United States is privately owned, and protecting species requires the cooperation of the landowners.

Percentage

- 0–20
- 20–40
- 40–60
- 60–80
- 80–90
- 90–100

Taken from: National Wilderness Institute

and other wildlife—until Europeans despoiled it. This concept seldom takes account of Native Americans. Indeed, when it mentions Native Americans it depicts them as primitive savages, sometimes as "ecologically noble savages."

The Myth of Former Abundance

My colleague Charles Kay, wildlife ecologist, has shown how serious a misconception this is. He has quantified all the wildlife observations and encounters with native people recorded in the journals of the [Meriwether] Lewis and [William] Clark expedition [of 1804 to 1806]. He found more than 40,000 journal entries and plotted the abundance of wildlife and native people day-by-day for the entire 863-day journey. The only places that Lewis and Clark observed significant numbers of wildlife were in buffer zones between tribes at war.

Because Indians avoided these zones, wild animals flourished. If it had not been for buffer zones, Lewis and Clark would have found little wildlife anywhere in the West. Kay's research demonstrates that humans were the apex predator in the pre-Columbian Americas. Along with new research in ecology, archeology, and anthropology, these findings clearly contradict the "nature undisturbed" vision.

Thus the current federal program to bring wolves to the West is based on a myth. At the time of Columbian contact, there were few wolves in the West. Humans, the top predators, out-competed wolves for their prey. Wolves only flourished after European crowd diseases decimated Native American populations. . . .

By concentrating on subpopulations and distinct population segments, managers miss an important point. What matters biologically is whether the DNA that represents a particular species continues to exist. Distinct DNA differences between subpopulations may offer a biological argument for preservation. Without those, however, there is little biological justification for federal expenditures.

The Role of Landowners

Third, the ESA is broken because it ignores one other important reality—that 80 percent of all listed species have all or part of their habitat on private land. Under the current law, landowners are punished for owning habitat that attracts or protects an endangered species. The act prohibits harm to an endangered species, and the Fish and Wildlife Service interprets harm to include modification of habitat.

Because modification of habitat equals "harm" in the eyes of the law, innocent people can be treated like wrong-doers. Once this interpretation was made, says Michael Bean of Environmental Defense, "a forest landowner harvesting timber, a farmer plowing new ground, or a developer clearing land for a shopping center potentially stood in the same position as a poacher taking aim at a whooping crane." This fact leads rational, normally law-abiding citizens to destroy habitat before an endangered species arrives.

What Ought to Be Done?

First, forget the 1970s' mythology and romanticism of the "balance of nature" and concentrate on real problems. Adopt environmental federalism as a clear policy goal—give state governments control over endangered species. The national government should be responsible for national problems, including the potential for global extinctions,

The government has launched conservation initiatives to preserve fish and wildlife near Hoover Dam while meeting the needs of local landowners.

not local ones. It makes little sense to spend scarce money to protect a marginal distinct subpopulation of a species already thriving elsewhere if it means you cannot protect an actual species from extinction. States can protect subspecies and distinct populations, using innovative techniques and creating interstate compacts for subspecies whose range crosses state lines.

Some will claim that if states are in control, they will neglect species protection in an attempt to promote economic development. In fact, the opposite tends to be true. State forests are better managed, both environmentally and economically, than federal forests. Some states have stricter laws than those imposed by the federal government.

Remove the Federal Hammer

My second recommendation is to take away federal officials' regulatory hammer and replace it with funding to encourage preservation. A simple administrative change could replace the definition of "harm" used by the Fish and Wildlife Service. Because "harm" currently includes habitat modification, federal agents have little incentive to be innovative in saving endangered species. But if they lose their regulatory hammer, they will have to discover new tools to protect species. . . .

To return to my three original themes: First, for at least 10,000 years humans have been the primary forces structuring "natural" systems, and those systems are in constant change. Saving species cannot rely on a "nature undisturbed" vision.

Second, we should leave national problems to the national government and leave distinct population segments or subpopulations to the states.

Third, the cooperation of landowners depends on changing the Endangered Species Act. Unless landowners can see that they will not be penalized in the future for providing space for species today, they will have no choice but to destroy habitat preemptively. . . .

These proposals actually are based on conservationist Aldo Leopold's admonition to experiment with many systems instead of following "one-track laws." By engaging property owners in the effort to protect species, we will also follow Leopold's admonition that "conservation will ultimately boil down to rewarding the private landowner who conserves the public interest." No claims about the value of biodiversity or moralizing about the diversity of life will change that basic fact.

EVALUATING THE AUTHOR'S ARGUMENTS:

In the viewpoint you have just read, the author argues that if landowners find an area on their land that would be a good place for an endangered species to live, these land-owners would conclude that the best thing to do is "destroy habitat before an endangered species arrives." Is it fair to restrict what private citizens can do with their own land in order to protect endangered species? How should a government balance the rights of landowners and the needs of species needing protection?

Viewpoint

3

The World's Fish Populations Are in Danger of Collapsing

"Estuaries, coral reefs, wetlands and oceanic fish were all 'rapidly losing populations, species, or entire functional groups.'"

Marla Cone

In the following viewpoint, journalist Martha Cone describes a study conducted by an international team of scientists, who conclude that, unless changes are made, human activities will cause many fish species to collapse by the year 2048. The authors of a report based on the study argue that the fishing industry is removing too many fish from the oceans, and that if trends continue, the ocean will not be able to recover and animals that eat fish will eventually be threatened as well.

Cone has covered environmental stories since 1985, and has published more than one thousand newspaper and magazine articles about human interactions with nature.

AS YOU READ, CONSIDER THE FOLLOWING QUESTIONS:

1. At what point is a fishery considered to have collapsed, according to the viewpoint?
2. As estimated by the National Fisheries Institute, how many metric tons of wild fish are taken each year?
3. What evidence is there that marine reserves and fishery closures are working to protect fish species?

All of the world's fishing stocks will collapse before midcentury, devastating food supplies, if overfishing and other human impacts continue at their current pace, according to a global study published today [November 3, 2006] by scientists in five countries.

Already, nearly one-third of species that are fished—including bluefin tuna, Atlantic cod, Alaskan king crab, Pacific salmon and an array in California fisheries—have collapsed, and the pace is accelerating, the report says.

If that trend continues, the study predicts that "100% of [fished] species will collapse by the year 2048, or around that," said marine biologist Boris Worm, who led the research team. A fishery is considered collapsed if catches fall to 10% of historic highs.

Without more protection soon, the world's ocean ecosystems won't be able to rebound from the shrinking populations of so many fish and other sea creatures, the scientists reported in the journal *Science*.

The report is the first comprehensive analysis of the potential consequences of ongoing declines in the oceans' diversity of life. In recent years, marine scientists have warned of the extreme toll of overfishing in many regions, but the new report, global in scope, offers one of the grimmest predictions for the future of the world's fisheries.

Yet there is hope, the scientists concluded: "Available data suggest that at this point, these trends are reversible."

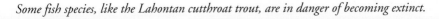

Some fish species, like the Lahontan cutthroat trout, are in danger of becoming extinct.

If more protections are put into place, such as new marine reserves and better-managed commercial fisheries, seafood supplies will surge and the oceans can recover, they said.

"The good news is that it is not too late to turn things around," said Worm, an assistant professor of marine conservation biology at Dalhousie University in Halifax, Canada. "It can be done, but it must be done soon. . . ."

Group Disputes Findings

A U.S. fishing industry group, the National Fisheries Institute, disputed the pessimistic findings, saying that fishermen and government already had acted and that federal data showed that "more than 80% of fish stocks are sustainable and will provide seafood now and for future generations."

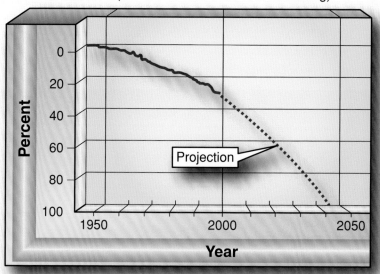

A Future Without Fish

A new study suggests that overfishing could lead to a catastrophic loss of marine species as soon as the middle of the century.

Percentage of species collapsed
(defined as less than 10% remaining)

Taken from: Cornelia Dean, "Study Sees 'Global Collapse' of Fish Species," *New York Times*, November 3, 2006

"Fish stocks naturally fluctuate in population. Fisheries scientists around the world actively manage stocks and rebuild fisheries with a low sustainable population," the institute said.

The group said that for the last 25 years, catches had been steady, with wild fisheries providing 85 million to 100 million metric tons annually and aquaculture—fish farming—helping to fill the growing demand.

The scientists, however, said they were confident of their predictions because they found "consistent agreement of theory, experiments, and observations across widely different scales and ecosystems."

"There's no question if we close our eyes and pretend it's all OK, it will continue along the same trajectory. Eventually, we're going to run out of species," Worm said.

Delving into recent catch data around the world as well as 1,000 years of historical archives in areas such as the San Francisco Bay, the team reported that estuaries, coral reefs, wetlands and oceanic fish were all "rapidly losing populations, species or entire functional groups."

Scarcity of a highly nutritious food supply for the world's growing human population would be the most visible effect of declining ocean species. But the scientists said other disruptions also were occurring as ocean ecosystems unraveled, species by species.

Biologists have long debated the lasting effect of removing a few species from oceans. The authors of the new report conclude that it sabotages oceans' stability and their recovery from stresses.

Other Effects

Water quality is worsening, and fish kills, toxic algal blooms, dead zones, invasive exotic species, beach closures and coastal floods are increasing, as wetlands, reefs and the animals and plants that filter pollutants disappear. Climate change also is altering marine ecosystems.

"Our analyses suggest that business as usual would foreshadow serious threats to global food security, coastal water quality and ecosystem stability, affecting current and future generations," the report says.

Not just humans, but other creatures are in danger of food shortages, biologists say.

"Animals like seals, dolphins and killer whales eat fish. If we strip the ocean of these kinds of species, other animals are going to suffer," said coauthor Stephen Palumbi of Stanford, who specializes in marine evolution and population biology. . . .

The new report documents "why ocean biodiversity matters," said Jane Lubchenco, an Oregon State University professor and member of the Pew Oceans Commission. "It's clear from the analysis that the problems are very real and getting worse, but—and here's the good news—that the downward spiral can be reversed."

The strength of the new report "lies in the breadth of the array of information the authors used for their analysis," said Andrew Sugden, *Science*'s international managing editor.

First, they analyzed 32 experiments that manipulated species in small areas and reported "a strikingly general picture": Decreased types of species spurred ecosystem-wide problems.

Also, the team assessed United Nations catch data since 1950 for all 64 of the Earth's large marine ecosystems, including the Bering Sea, California Current and Gulf of Mexico.

FAST FACT

For more than 1 billion people worldwide, fish is the major source of protein, according to the environmental program of the Pew Charitable Trust.

Changes in native species were also tracked over a 1,000-year period in 12 coastal regions, including San Francisco, Chesapeake and Galveston bays. About 91% suffered at least a 50% decline, and 7% were extinct.

Mirroring Declines

Worm said similarities in all the data "surprised, even shocked" him and his colleagues. The smallest experiments—a few square meters—mirrored the declines seen in ocean basins.

Palumbi warned that "this century is the last century of wild seafood" unless there are fundamental changes in managing ocean ecosystems.

At 48 areas already protected by marine reserves and fishery closures in California, Florida, the Philippines, the Caribbean and elsewhere, species declines reversed and catches nearby increased fourfold, the study says.

Coauthor Heike Lotze, also of Dalhousie University, reported in June [2006] that "human history rather than natural change" drove declines.

"Overfishing is almost certainly the most important factor, but habitat destruction, pollution and climate change may also contribute," Worm said.

EVALUATING THE AUTHOR'S ARGUMENTS:

In this viewpoint, the primary challenge to the scientists' findings comes from the National Fisheries Institute, a group that represents commercial fishers in the United States. How should a reader weigh the opinions of the scientists and of the fishers? What does each group stand to gain or to lose from this debate?

The Threat of Fish Population Collapse Is Greatly Exaggerated

Kevin Howe and Sarah C.P. Williams

"We as fishermen see how much fish there is, and we've been catching a lot more fish than ever before."

In the following viewpoint, Kevin Howe and Sarah C.P. Williams present arguments that widely publicized claims about an impending collapse of fish populations are greatly exaggerated. They note that scientists report that the amount of fish harvested has been in decline, but that professional fishers have observed just the opposite. The real threat, they conclude, is to the fishing industry, which is forced to work under increasing governmental regulations designed to counteract imagined environmental dangers.

Kevin Howe is a staff writer for the *Monterey County Herald.* Sarah C.P. Williams is a science-writing intern at the Stanford University School of Medicine.

1. According to the report in the journal *Science*, when might the world's fisheries collapse?
2. Why does Monterey, California, show fewer signs of declining fish populations, as explained by marine ecologist Steve Palumbi?
3. Why is the number of fishing vessels declining, according to the viewpoint?

The sky isn't falling and the fish will still be around in mid-century, according to fishermen and critics of a recent article that forecast a bleak future for the fishing industry.

The article, published Nov. 3 [2006] in the magazine *Science*, predicted the collapse of all of the world's fisheries by 2048, based on declining fish harvest numbers and other research. It also sparked a firestorm of controversy, generating headlines nationwide in newspapers and news magazines, spinning off into an elaborately illustrated feature in *Time* magazine.

Among critics like Ray Hilborn, a peer review scientist at the University of Washington, the article was "probably the most absurd prediction that's ever appeared in a scientific journal regarding fisheries."

Hilborn called the *Science* article findings "silly," but also worried that they "will become completely accepted in the ecological community. They have no skepticism."

But the researchers who wrote the *Science* story—including two from Stanford University's Hopkins Marine Station in Pacific Grove, Calif.—are sticking to their findings.

"I haven't seen any science that shows we're wrong," said Steve Palumbi, a marine ecologist at Hopkins. "There are opinions I've heard, but I haven't seen any science." . . .

A Growing Trend

At the core of the controversy is what critics call the growing "enviro-sensationalism" trend of environmental news, said Steve Ralston, senior fishery biologist with the National Oceanic and Atmospheric Administration's National Marine Fisheries Office in Santa Cruz [California].

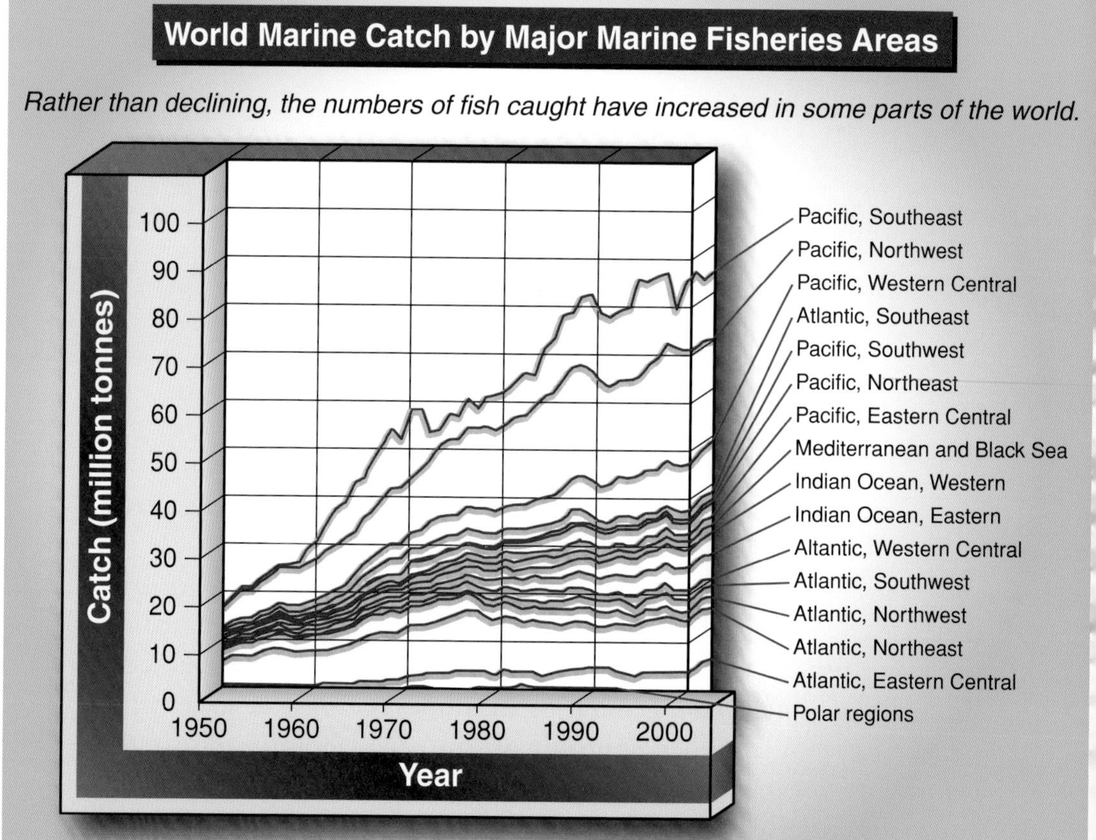
World Marine Catch by Major Marine Fisheries Areas
Rather than declining, the numbers of fish caught have increased in some parts of the world.
Catch (million tonnes)
100
90
80
70
60
50
40
30
20
10
0
1950
1960
1970
1980
1990
2000
Year
Pacific, Southeast
Pacific, Northwest
Pacific, Western Central
Atlantic, Southeast
Pacific, Southwest
Pacific, Northeast
Pacific, Eastern Central
Mediterranean and Black Sea
Indian Ocean, Western
Indian Ocean, Eastern
Altantic, Western Central
Atlantic, Southwest
Atlantic, Northwest
Atlantic, Northeast
Atlantic, Eastern Central
Polar regions

Taken from: FAO (Food and Agriculture Organization of the United Nations)

He referred to the growing number of similar reports as "an increasing 'Chicken Little' response."

The principal objection, Ralston said, is that the scientists infer that fisheries are going to "collapse" based on declining catches.

But one reason for the decline, he said, has been a successful management program. "The basic way they measure 'collapse' is flawed. Catch is not a good way to measure the status of the fish stock."

The authors of the original paper acknowledged that there is some validity to Ralston's argument.

"Yes, catches are an imperfect measure of the stock abundance," said lead author Boris Worm, a marine biologist at Canada's Dalhousie University. He said, however, that declines in catches are still indicative of larger trends.

"It's obvious that when the catches collapse, it's often because there's no more fish to be found," Worm said.

Critics of the research have also cited the successful recovery of some fish populations, like rockfish, as evidence against decline. . . .

"I'm very disappointed in *Science* magazine," Ralston said. "This is not the first article that's almost created a panic situation with ocean resources and fish."

Hilborn said many of the world's fisheries are not well managed and are getting worse, but the United States, Iceland, New Zealand, Australia and others have successfully pursued strategies to keep fisheries sustainable. For instance, those countries are getting rid of a fishing industry race that led fishermen to build and operate ever-bigger boats to bring in ever-bigger catches.

Lowering the take, he said, is the key.

Ralston describes himself as "an ardent conservationist," but said he worries that public exaggerations of environmental problems erode the credibility of scientists and the conservation movement.

Fishers view the *Science* report as another undeserved slap at them and their industry.

"I see a completely different picture of fishing and the ocean," said Jiri Nozicka of Monterey, Calif., a native of the Czech Republic and a fisherman on Monterey Bay for the past seven years.

"We as fishermen see how much fish there is, and we've been catching a lot more fish than ever before."

Palumbi acknowledged that some areas of the world have not seen such drastic declines in fish populations as others. In fact, a main point of the paper was that the collapse in fish numbers is dependent on the diversity of ecosystems.

"In Monterey," he said, "we're in a hotspot of diversity. So the collapse is happening more slowly here." The research, however, looked at the global picture.

FAST FACT

A fifteen-year study led by the Scripps Institute of Oceanography at the University of California, San Diego, showed that 2004 populations of fish living in the deepest parts of the Pacific Ocean had increased to three times their 1989 numbers.

Fishers Are the Endangered Species

Fishermen have also said the study was flawed because catch numbers are influenced by government regulations.

"There's huge waste created by reduced limits by the federal government because of quotas not matching reality," said Joe Pennisi, Nozicka's brother-in-law and fishing partner.

Fishers, Nozicka said, are forced to throw catches overboard because of regulations limiting the number of fish they can land, and that lowers the landing numbers scientists rely on to determine fish population.

In addition to the lower catch limits, he said, the number of fishing vessels is also declining. If there's an endangered species on the coast, Nozicka said, it's the American fisher.

A fishing industry can collapse, he said, when there are too few boats on the water to support the fish canning and processing industries, not to mention the businesses ashore that maintain, supply, build, fuel, service and sell boats.

The decline in fishers, however, is also closely tied to the number of fish in the ocean, say some scientists.

Some people believe that it may no longer be necessary to preserve underwater species by releasing new fish into lakes and rivers.

"Historically, the cause of a shrinking fishing industry is because of declining stock," [Fiorenzo] Micheli [a scientist at Hopkins Marine Station and a coauthor of the *Science* article] said.

Jared Roth, who was until recently an observer for National Oceanic and Atmospheric Administration's West Coast Groundfish Observer Program, disagreed.

"There's a lot of fish out there," Roth said. "Nobody knows what's down there, and that might always be the case. The ocean is really mysterious; it's dark, always changing. It's really hard to know what the truth is down there." . . .

Roth, too, worries about the future of the industry, which he sees as a fleet of aging boats and aging skippers, with few young people willing to come in the business.

"Fishing is so hard, really hard," he said. When people set out to harvest wild fish on a wild ocean "you really have to be able to adapt, to have lots of options, to be lucky, smart, skilled and tough."

"People don't value the resource," he said. "If they really knew where their food was coming from and wanted real local fresh food, then these guys wouldn't so easily be weeded out. We should be valuing these guys. What will replace these guys? They seem to be going out of style fast, like family farms."

This is one point that all the scientists agree on.

EVALUATING THE AUTHORS' ARGUMENTS:

The viewpoint you have just read exposes a conflict between the commercial fishing industry and some environmentalists. People who fish for a living believe that they are able to assess how healthy fish populations are and to make good decisions about how many fish to take in order to preserve the health of those populations. Some environmentalists believe that evaluating population trends is best left to scientists and that setting limits for how many fish to catch is best left to government. How do you think these evaluations and rules should be made? Explain your answer.

Polar Bears Are Threatened by Global Warming

Kassie Siegel

"Absent cuts in greenhouse gas emissions . . . the polar bear may disappear entirely in less than 40 years."

In the viewpoint that follows, Kassie Siegel argues that unless steps are taken quickly to reduce greenhouse gas emissions, global warming will cause crucial habitat to melt, which in turn will pose a serious threat to polar bears. With the loss of sea ice, she explains, polar bears find it more difficult to hunt and to care for young, and some populations of the bears have already begun to decline. There is not much time, she concludes, to make the changes that could save polar bears and other threatened species.

Siegel is a staff attorney at the Center for Biological Diversity, a conservation organization working to protect endangered animals and plants.

AS YOU READ, CONSIDER THE FOLLOWING QUESTIONS:

1. Why, according to the author, will the polar bear being listed as a threatened species lead to reduction in the emissions of greenhouse gases?
2. According to the journal *Arctic*, why are more polar bears being found on land near human settlements?
3. According to one study cited by the author, what portion of the earth's creatures may be extinct by the year 2050?

Kassie Siegel, "The Tip of the Iceberg; The Polar Bear Isn't the Only Creature Facing a Bleak Feature because of Global Warming," *Los Angeles Times*, January 8, 2007. Reproduced by permission of the author.

O n Dec. 27 [2006], Interior Secretary Dirk Kempthorne announced a proposal to list the polar bear as a threatened species under the Endangered Species Act because of the loss of its sea ice habitat from global warming. This proposal marks the first legally binding admission by the [President George W.] Bush administration of the reality of global warming. The significance of the polar bear decision has not been missed by those who stand to benefit from a continuation of the administration's head-in-the-sand approach to global warming. Once protection for the polar bear is finalized, federal agencies and other large greenhouse gas emitters will be required by law to ensure that their emissions do not jeopardize the species. And the only way to avoid jeopardizing the polar bear is to reduce emissions.

Predictably, opponents of emissions cuts are doing what they have always done: claim a scientific dispute where none exists and urge that

Polar bears live in the northern Arctic regions.

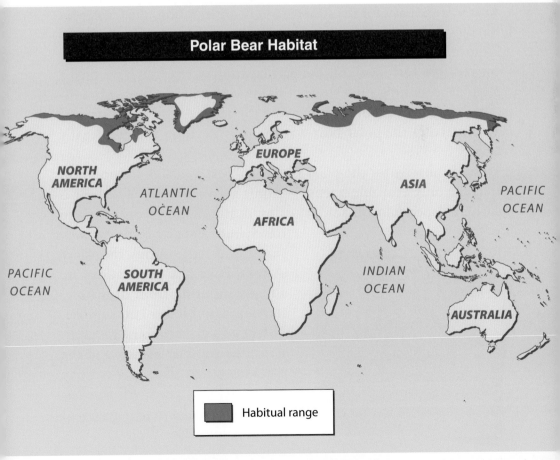

Polar Bear Habitat

NORTH AMERICA

EUROPE

ASIA

PACIFIC OCEAN

ATLANTIC OCEAN

AFRICA

PACIFIC OCEAN

SOUTH AMERICA

INDIAN OCEAN

AUSTRALIA

Habitual range

no action be taken until the science is "conclusive." Singing this tired tune, an editorial in the *Wall Street Journal* last week called the proposal to protect polar bears a "triumph of politics over science," arguing that polar bears are "overly abundant" and that the species cannot be considered threatened until its population has further declined.

The *Journal* got it wrong in every respect. What is remarkable about the polar bear decision is that it is a rare case of science actually triumphing over politics, not the other way around. From burying the National Assessment of Climate Change Impacts on the United States to trying to gag top NASA [National Aeronautics and Space Administration] climate scientist James Hansen, the Bush administration has systematically attempted to suppress science on global warming.

"Best Available Science"

However, the "best available science" standard required by the Endangered Species Act forbids political and economic considerations. That was the basis for the strategy of my organization, the Center for Biological Diversity, when, on Feb. 16, 2005 (the same day the Kyoto Protocol [an international treaty regulating greenhouse gas emissions] entered into force without the participation of the U.S.), we filed a petition requesting protection of the polar bear. The Bush administration could refuse only by denying the science of global warming. So protecting the polar bear was the only decision it could legally make.

Unfortunately for the polar bear, the "best available science"—in fact, the only available science—paints a grim picture. The bear is entirely dependent on sea ice, using it as a platform on which to travel, hunt and give birth. Yet each year, as the Arctic warms, the sea ice shrinks. Polar bear populations are already suffering from drowning, starvation and lower cub survival. Absent cuts in greenhouse gas emissions, the summer sea ice, and the polar bear, may disappear entirely in less than 40 years. All this has been documented in peer-reviewed scientific journals.

> **FAST FACT**
>
> For every week during the summer that a polar bear cannot hunt from sea ice, the bear loses twenty to forty pounds of stored fat that is needed to sustain it through the winter.

Studies show that polar bear numbers are declining due to food shortages resulting from earlier summer ice melts.

Notwithstanding the scientific consensus that polar bears are threatened with extinction because of global warming, there will always be fossil fuel-addicted naysayers misrepresenting reality. Just as the tobacco industry could always find a "scientist" to claim that there was no link between smoking and lung cancer, climate-change deniers such as Sen. James M. Inhofe (R-Okla.) will always find polar bear population numbers and trends that purport to prove that the species is doing fine.

More polar bears are being seen near human settlements in Canada, they say, therefore polar bear populations must be increasing. Wrong. A study by NASA and Canadian Wildlife Service scientists published in September 2006 in the journal *Arctic* demonstrated that more polar bears were indeed being seen on land—not because the species was "overly-abundant" but because the bears had nowhere else to go. They should be out on the ice hunting seals, but earlier breakup of sea ice means the bears are stuck on land, where they are more likely to be spotted.

Global Warming and Population Decline

Inhofe and the *Wall Street Journal* would take no action to protect polar bears until their population has declined significantly. But five of the 19 distinct polar bear populations are already known to be declining. And given the undisputed trajectory of sea ice retreat, the species must still be considered threatened even if there were not yet any evidence of population decline. If a ship starts taking on water, you don't wait until the first passenger drowns before issuing a mayday; the passengers are clearly "threatened" as soon as the water starts pouring in.

But polar bears are not the first species (nor will they likely be the last) for which we have sought the protections of the Endangered Species Act because of global warming. The first, in 2001, was the Kittlitz's murrelet, a small seabird that feeds at the mouth of tidewater glaciers and whose decline corresponds to the global-warming-induced retreat of those glaciers.

Alas, the eyes of the world did not turn to the plight of the Kittlitz's murrelet, as we had hoped, and the administration quietly refused to protect it, a decision we are challenging in court. In 2004, we filed a petition seeking protection for the staghorn and elkhorn corals, species that have declined by more than 90% because of a host of threats, including global warming. The corals were listed as threatened species in May [2006], but with far less fanfare than the polar bear and without an explicit recognition of global warming as a cause of their decline. In November [2006], we petitioned to protect 12 penguin species, including the ice-dependent emperor penguin.

These species are, unfortunately, just the tip of the extinction iceberg. One study estimates that a third of the Earth's creatures will be condemned to extinction by 2050. Polar bears may not be extinct until 2040, but that doesn't mean we have 30 years to do nothing.

EVALUATING THE AUTHOR'S ARGUMENTS:

The author of the viewpoint you have just read uses mildly mocking language to characterize the people who disagree with her: She refers to the federal government's "head-in-the-sand approach to global warming" and describes an argument against her position as a "tired tune." How does this kind of language affect the way you respond to the viewpoint? Explain your answer.

Polar Bears Are Not Threatened by Global Warming

James Inhofe

> *"There are more polar bears in the world now than there were 40 years ago."*

The following viewpoint was originally a speech presented in January 2007 by U.S. senator James Inhofe to the Senate Committee on Environment and Public Works. In his speech, Inhofe argues that there is no scientific reason to list polar bears as a threatened species under the federal Endangered Species Act. He contends that rather than declining, the number of polar bears is stable. Further, Inhofe concludes, any argument that the bears need to be protected because of climate-induced melting is premature, because it has not been proven that global warming is happening at all.

Inhofe is a Republican senator from Oklahoma. In 2006 he was voted the "Most Outstanding Conservative U.S. Senator" by the newspaper *Human Events* and the American Conservative Union.

Senator James Inhofe, "The Polarizing Politics of the Polar Bear," Speech to U.S. Senate Committee on Environment and Public Works, January 4, 2007. http://epw.senate.gov/public/index.cfm?FuseAction=Press Room.Speeches&ContentRecord_id=ef3ad1ff-802a-23ad-496d-dc3b128db3ce&Region_id=&Issue_id

Mr. President, I rise today [January 4, 2007] to address the U.S. Fish and Wildlife Service's recent action to begin formal consideration of whether to list the polar bear as a threatened species under the Endangered Species Act (ESA). Over the next year, the Fish and Wildlife Service will examine scientific and commercial data regarding the health of the polar bear population and evaluate the presence of any threats to its existence.

The question that the Fish and Wildlife Service must answer is: Is there clear, scientific evidence that current worldwide polar bear populations are in trouble and facing possible extinction in the foreseeable future?

As the Fish and Wildlife Service reviews the issue over the next year, I feel confident they will conclude as I have, that listing the polar bear is unwarranted.

In the proposal, the Fish and Wildlife Service acknowledges that for seven of the 19 worldwide polar bear populations, the Service has no population trend data of any kind. Other data suggest that for an additional five polar bear populations, the number of bears is not declining and is stable. Two more of the bear populations showed reduced numbers in the past due to over hunting, but these two populations are now increasing because of hunting restrictions.

Other sources of data mentioned in a recent *Wall Street Journal* piece suggest that "there are more polar bears in the world now than there were 40 years ago." The Fish and Wildlife Service estimates that the polar bear population is 20,000 to 25,000 bears, whereas in the 1950s and 1960s, estimates were as low as 5,000–10,000 bears due to sport hunting, which has since been restricted.

A 2002 U.S. Geological Survey of wildlife in the Arctic Refuge Coastal Plain noted that the polar bear populations "may now be near historic highs."

The Endangered Species Act Is Broken

So if the number of polar bears does not appear to be in decline, why are we considering listing the species as threatened? Because the ESA is broken and this proposal is indicative of what is wrong with it.

Not everyone agrees that global warming presents a threat to polar bears.

The ESA allows the Service to list the entire range of polar bears as threatened and thereby extend a wide array of regulatory restrictions to them and their habitat, despite a dearth of data and the lack of scientific evidence that polar bears are indeed in trouble.

The law also allows for the Fish and Wildlife Service to justify its proposal on a sample from a single population in Western Hudson Bay in Canada, where bear populations have decreased by 259 polar bears in the last 17 years. Yet hunting was allowed during that entire period in the Western Hudson Bay population. In fact, according to the latest figures collected by the International Union for Conservation of Nature and Natural Resources, 234 bears have been killed in the last 5 years alone. How many more were killed in the previous 12 years and what overall affect did this have on population numbers?

Ironically, the Canadian government is right now considering a proposal to increase the quota on the harvesting of polar bears in the Western Hudson Bay population. This would allow more hunting of the population whose condition is so dire that the Service based its listing decision on it. While I support hunting as a general matter, we need to fully understand its impact on the polar bear populations before we blame global warming for changes in bear populations.

Hypothetical Climate Change

The Fish and Wildlife Service asserts that the reason for the decline in the Western Hudson Bay population is climate-change-induced ice melting. To make that assertion, they rely on hypothetical climate change computer models showing massive loss of ice that irreparably damages the polar bear's habitat. The Service then extrapolates that reasoning to the other 18 populations of polar bears, making the assumption that all bears in these populations will eventually decline and go extinct. Again, this conclusion is not based on field data but on hypothetical modeling and that is considered perfectly acceptable "scientific evidence" under the ESA.

> **FAST FACT**
>
> The United States is one of the signers of the 1973 treaty called the Agreement on the Conservation of Polar Bears. The other countries that signed the treaty are Canada, Russia, Norway, and Denmark.

Polar Bear Population Estimates

Polar bear populations have grown steadily since the 1950s.

1950s	5,000
1965–1970	8,000–10,000
1984	25,000
2005	20,000–25,000

Taken from: "Polar Bear Politics," *Wall Street Journal*, January 3, 2007

I do not believe our federal conservation policy should be dictated by hypothetical computer projections because the stakes of a listing decision under ESA can be extremely high. The listing of the polar bear is no exception. . . .

Furthermore because the Fish and Wildlife Service has linked the ice flow habitat concerns of polar bears to global climate change, all kinds of projects around the country could be challenged. Some will say that this is not possible or that I'm exaggerating. But if you take the ESA to its logical conclusion, which is certain to be done by environmental special interests, any activity that allegedly affects climate change or greenhouse gas emissions may have to be evaluated and approved by Fish and Wildlife Service for its effect on the ice flows on which polar bears depend. Thus, this proposal could be the ultimate assault on local land use decision-making and suppression of private property rights to date.

So it is important that we take the next year to gather and critically evaluate more science about these impressive creatures to determine whether or not they really are in trouble. We need to replace speculation and uncertainty with facts and figures. I look forward to working with the Fish and Wildlife Service on this important listing decision and I firmly believe that the science will show that the evidence pointing to a threat to polar bears is not sufficient to warrant federal ESA protection and all the regulatory land use control that comes with it.

EVALUATING THE AUTHOR'S ARGUMENTS:

James Inhofe argues that the federal government should not step in to protect polar bears from extinction due to global warming, because the threat of global warming itself has not yet been proven conclusively. How do you think governments should respond to potential dangers? Is it fair to ask citizens to restrict their activities because of something that might happen in the future?

Chapter 2

Are Efforts to Help Endangered Species Effective?

PETA activists stage protests to raise awareness about the importance of preserving animals in threatened situations.

The Endangered Species Act Saves Species from Extinction

A Letter from Biologists

"The ESA has served our nation well, largely because of its flexibility and its solid foundation in science."

The following viewpoint was originally an open letter from a group of concerned scientists. On March 8, 2006, the letter, signed by 5,738 biologists, was hand delivered to the U.S. Senate to provide expert advice as the Senate debated the fate of the Endangered Species Act. In the letter, the biologists argue that the Endangered Species Act has been effective at protecting species, largely because the Act has been governed by solid scientific principles. It is important, they conclude, that the act be allowed to continue protecting species, by maintaining adequate funding and a reliance on science-based recovery plans.

AS YOU READ, CONSIDER THE FOLLOWING QUESTIONS:

1. Who was president of the United States when the Endangered Species Act became law, according to the viewpoint?
2. Since the Endangered Species Act was passed in 1973, what percentage of species have made a complete recovery, as reported in the viewpoint?

3. According to the viewpoint, what new threats to native species diversity have been identified since the Endangered Species Act was passed?

Dear Senators:

We are writing as biologists with expertise in a variety of scientific disciplines that concern biological diversity and the loss of species. With the Senate considering policies that could have long-lasting impacts on this nation's species diversity, we ask that you take into account scientific principles that are crucial to species conservation. Biological diversity provides food, fiber, medicines, clean water, and myriad other ecosystem products and services on which we depend every day. If we look only at well-studied species groups, nearly one-third of native species in the United States are at risk of disappearing. Extinction is truly irreversible—once gone, individual species and all of the services that they provide us cannot be brought back.

On December 8, 1973, President Richard Nixon signed the Endangered Species Act ("ESA") with the goal of conserving endangered and threatened species and the ecosystems on which they depend. For species that have been listed and provided protection under the ESA, much of that purpose has been achieved. According to an article in the September 30, 2005, edition of *Science*, less than one percent of listed species have gone extinct since 1973, while 10 percent of candidate species still waiting to be listed have suffered that fate. In addition to the hundreds of species that the Act has protected from extinction, listing has contributed to population increases or the stabilization of populations for at least 35 percent of listed species, and perhaps significantly more, as well as the

The bald eagle, whose numbers in the wild are growing, is a species that was restored through the protections of the Endangered Species Act.

recovery of such signature species as the peregrine falcon. While complete recovery has been realized for just two percent of species listed, given the precarious state of most species when listed, this represents significant progress.

One of the great strengths of the Endangered Species Act is its foundation in sound scientific principles and its reliance on the best available science. Unfortunately, recent legislative proposals would critically weaken this foundation. For species conservation to continue, it is imperative both that the scientific principles embodied in the Act are maintained, and that the Act is strengthened, fully implemented, and adequately funded.

Listing
Objective scientific information and methods should be used in listing species, subspecies, and distinct population segments as endangered or threatened under the Act. While non-scientific factors may appropriately be considered at points later in the process of protecting

species, their use in listing decisions is inconsistent with biologically defensible principles. Due to the fragile state of many of those species that require the Act's protections, the listing process needs to proceed as promptly as possible; otherwise, species will go extinct while waiting to be listed.

Habitat

Habitat provides the unique food, shelter, and other complex requirements that each species needs for its survival; habitat loss and degradation are the principal reasons for the decline of most species at risk. Habitat protection is essential if species are to be conserved and the goals of the ESA are to be met. The relationship between species, their habitats, and the threats they face can be exceedingly complex.

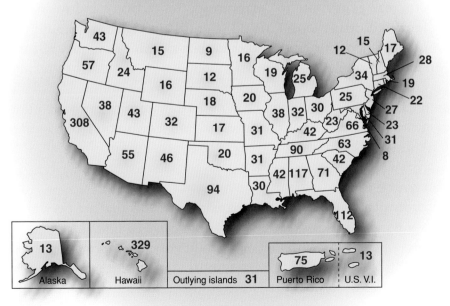

Numbers of Threatened and Endangered Species by State and Territory

The Endangered Species Act protects endangered and threatened species in every state and territory in the United States.

Taken from: U.S. Fish and Wildlife Service, updated March 20, 2007

Therefore, the chances of species recovery are maximized when habitat protection is based on sound scientific principles, and when the determinations of the biological needs of at-risk species are scientifically well informed.

The obligation for federal agencies to consult with the appropriate wildlife agency and its biologists when federal actions could affect habitat for listed species is an indispensable provision in the ESA. It provides the means for science to inform decisions about the habitat-dependent survival and recovery of species at-risk. The designation of critical habitat places further obligations on the Federal government to, among other things, protect the habitat essential to species recovery. It is far more effective, far easier, and far less expensive to protect functioning natural habitats than it is to recreate them once they are gone.

Scientific Tools

The current Endangered Species Act standard of "best available science" has worked well and has been flexible enough over time to accommodate evolving scientific information and practice. Failure to keep the ESA open to the use of scientific information from the best available research and monitoring, and to rely on impartial scientific experts, will contribute to delays in species recovery and to species declines and extinctions. Critical scientific information should not only include current empirical data, but also, for example, historic habitat and population information, population surveys, habitat and population modeling, and taxonomic and genetic studies. Use of scientific knowledge should not be hampered by administrative requirements that overburden or slow the Act's implementation, or by limiting consideration of certain types of scientific information.

Recovery Plans

Recovery plans must be science-based documents that are developed with the input of scientists and are responsive to new information. Recovery plans must be based on the best possible information about the specific biology of each species, must identify threats to each species and address what is needed to mitigate those threats, and must predict how species are likely to respond to mitigation measures that may be adopted. To be most effective, recovery plans need to incorporate scientific principles of adaptive management, so they can be updated as new information on species and their habitats becomes available. Changes to the ESA that would delay completion of recovery plans, or provide for inflexible recovery goals that cannot be informed by new or additional scientific knowledge, should be avoided.

Scientific Advances and New Issues

The scientific community has contributed significant new information on imperiled species, their uses of habitats, and threats to those resources since the ESA was first passed into law. Serious, new, and as yet insufficiently addressed issues, such as global warming and invasive species, have emerged as primary environmental concerns that affect the fate of our native species diversity. We urge Congress to initiate thorough studies to consider the foremost problems that drive species toward extinction.

Losing species means losing the potential to solve some of humanity's most intractable problems, including hunger and disease. The Endangered Species Act is more than just a law—it is the ultimate safety net in our life support system. As Earth has changed and as science has progressed since the Endangered Species Act was authorized in 1973, the ESA has served our nation well, largely because of its flexibility and its solid foundation in science. It is crucial to maintain these fundamental principles.

EVALUATING THE AUTHORS' ARGUMENTS:

The viewpoint you have just read was written by a group of biologists and addressed to U.S. senators who probably have, as a group, limited education in science. What steps do the biologists take to emphasize their superior knowledge of the scientific issues involved in protecting species? Why, for example, are the words "science" and "scientific" repeated so many times throughout the viewpoint?

The Endangered Species Act Is Not Effective at Saving Species from Extinction

"We may not be able to address the species that biologically have the most significant threats."

Sandy Bauers

In the following viewpoint, Sandy Bauers, a staff writer at the *Philadelphia Inquirer*, analyzes the federal government's listing of "candidate" species, or species that are being considered for protection as threatened or endangered. The process of moving a species from list to list is so cumbersome, critics argue, that many species become extinct before they can be saved. The viewpoint concludes that the Endangered Species Act is much less effective than it otherwise could be because it is so complicated and the process is so expensive.

AS YOU READ, CONSIDER THE FOLLOWING QUESTIONS:
1. As described in the viewpoint, what is a red knot?
2. According to the Center for Biological Diversity, how many species have become extinct while they were on the "candidate" list?
3. How does the number of listings under President George W. Bush compare with the listings under the presidents who came before him, according to the viewpoint?

When a new list of species worthy of federal protection came out recently, the howls of protest were not about the ones that didn't make the list.

They were about the ones that did.

The U.S. Fish and Wildlife Service added seven species to a list now totaling 279 "candidates"—those that warrant federal protection but are a few procedural steps away from being declared threatened or endangered.

The additions are two Florida butterflies, two Alabama snails, the pricklyapple cactus, the New England cottontail, and the red knot, a shorebird that alights on Delaware Bay beaches every spring to refuel on crab eggs.

While the list gives a species in trouble a bit more cachet and a dribble of federal money, critics say it is a death trap. Once on the list, few species graduate to the next level and get the full legal muscle that goes with being declared threatened or endangered.

The candidate list, released Sept. 12 [2006], "gives the appearance of action without really taking any," said the American Bird Conservancy's Perry Plumart, who has prowled meetings and stalked decision-makers for years to plead the case of the red knot.

The List Is Ineffective

"Policy purgatory," echoed New Jersey Audubon's Eric Stiles.

"It's essentially where species go to die," said Jason Rylander, staff lawyer with Defenders of Wildlife.

According to a study by the Center for Biological Diversity, 24 candidate species did just that while they awaited a boost to threatened or endangered.

One species the center identified as having gone extinct while on the list is Guam's cardinal honey-eater. The governor of the U.S. territory petitioned the service to list it in 1979, and it was made a candidate in 1982. It has not been seen since 1984.

On average, said the Tucson, Ariz.–based environmental group, species linger on the list 17 years.

That is time the red knot does not have. A computer model has predicted the bird could be extinct within four years.

The New England cottontail is teetering as well. Its geographic range has declined 85 percent since 1960.

Many groups protest the decision to either allow or disallow the listing of a species through the Endangered Species Act.

John Litvaitis, a professor at the University of New Hampshire, said full federal protection—not just the candidate list—was the "key to survival."

Defending the List

Others, however, say the list works. In fact, Jaret Daniels, a butterfly expert with the University of Florida, said full federal protection might be too cumbersome for the two Florida butterflies that were recently made candidates.

The butterflies, the Florida leafwing and Bartram's hairstreak, have been reduced to isolated populations in just two locations.

The red knot comes to Delaware Bay partway through an epic migration from the tip of South America to the Arctic. The fat-rich eggs it depends on to gain enough weight to resume the trip are those of the horseshoe crab.

The crabs, however, are used as bait for conch, a delicacy in Asia. With an increase in the crab harvest, numbers of red knots on the bay have plummeted from nearly 100,000 in the 1990s to just 13,000.

"Falling Down"

Last spring, New Jersey halted the crab harvest for two years, but surrounding states still allow a limited harvest. Delaware is considering new restrictions.

Conservationists now see the red knot as emblematic of problems within the Fish and Wildlife Service.

"I think the service is falling down on the job," Plumart said. "The reality is that the bird is in danger of winking out."

A main problem, the service and its critics agree, is money.

In 2005, the research, public hearings and other requirements to propel a species to the threatened or endangered lists cost as much as $300,000, according to the service.

And what money the service does have—$5.1 million for listings this year—is siphoned off by legal expenses.

High Vickery, a spokesman for the Interior Department, said the legal floodgates opened after a 1997 provision of the Endangered Species Act that required that a "critical habitat" be mapped before a species could be listed.

The process was so complicated and contentious, he said, that it became a "litigation magnet."

Lawsuits and Lack of Will

Responding to lawsuits "automatically trumps" other work, said Valerie Fellows, a spokeswoman for the Fish and Wildlife Service. As a result, she said, "we may not be able to address the species that biologically have the most significant threats. That's become the nature of the beast."

It has become a Catch-22 [a no-win situation]. The service is so preoccupied with suits challenging its failure to list a species that the only way to get a species listed may be to sue.

As of January [2006], the service was embroiled in 31 lawsuits, was subject to 56 court orders, and was responding to 26 notices of intent to sue, Fellows said.

FAST FACT

Since the Endangered Species Act became law in 1973, almost thirteen hundred species in the United States have been listed as endangered or threatened. Of these, fewer than 1 percent have recovered enough to be removed from the list.

"Right now," Vickery said, "you've got lawyers and judges setting the agenda for the Fish and Wildlife Service rather than professional biologists."

Audubon's Stiles says he sees no way around it. "The only tool we have left as a conservation community is to litigate," he said. "It's unfortunate."

Critics say there is also a lack of political will to list species.

Based on data from the Fish and Wildlife Service, the Center for Biological Diversity has determined that listings under the [President George W. Bush] administration have averaged 10 species a year, compared with 65 a year during the [President Bill] Clinton administration and 59 a year during [President] George H. W. Bush's administration.

Conservationists say the Act can work. Of 1,346 domestic species designated as threatened or endangered since the 1973 Act was passed, 11 have recovered enough to be delisted. Eight have gone extinct.

It's "an effective tool for preventing extinction," said Noah Greenwald, a biologist with the Center. "But it can only save the species if they're actually designated as threatened or endangered."

EVALUATING THE AUTHOR'S ARGUMENTS:

Woven through the viewpoint you have just read is the story of the red knot, a species that conservationists say may be in danger of becoming extinct within a few years. How much does it matter that most people may have never even heard of or seen the bird in question? What steps does the author of the viewpoint take to suggest the importance of the bird, cactus, snails, and other species she mentions?

Tiger Farms Might Rescue Endangered Cats

John Nielsen

"Wild tigers may already be doomed, so why not gamble with the farming plan?"

In the following viewpoint, John Nielsen describes a new plan to save tigers from extinction: Raise tigers in captivity on farms, and sell their bodies to makers of traditional medicines when the animals die naturally. Selling dead tigers legally, proponents argue, would take away the reason that hunters kill tigers in the wild, because there would be plenty of tiger parts available on the open market. Although there are risks involved with the plan, supporters of tiger farms worry that it may be the only chance left to save the tiger.

John Nielsen covers environmental issues for National Public Radio. He is the author of *Condor: To the Brink and Back–The Life and Times of One Giant Bird* (2006).

AS YOU READ, CONSIDER THE FOLLOWING QUESTIONS:
1. What parts of the tiger are used in traditional Asian medicines, as reported in the viewpoint?
2. How could former tiger poachers earn a living if there was no longer a market for their illegally obtained tiger parts, according to Barun Mitra's plan?

Conservation experts say the wild tiger may be headed for extinction. Twenty years ago, there were tens of thousands of these big cats in the wild. Today, there may be fewer than 3,000.

One of the biggest threats to wild tigers is poachers, who kill the animals with snares and poisons. Almost every part of a tiger can be sold. But by most accounts, it's the booming black market for traditional Asian medicines, such as tiger-blood wine and powdered tiger bone, that keep the poachers in business. Attempts to close this market by cracking down on poachers and banning products made from tiger parts have failed, especially in China.

Radical Step

Some conservationists say it's time to take a radical step to save the wild tigers: Legalize the sale of tiger bones and organs taken from the carcasses of big cats raised on Chinese tiger farms.

"There are roughly 4,000 tigers living on these farms, which means about 300 to 400 tigers die a natural death each year," said Barun Mitra of the free market Liberty Institute in New Dehli, India. "The question is: What do you do with their bones and carcasses?"

FAST FACT

According to the Tiger Missing Link Foundation, there are approximately 8,977 tigers in captivity in the United States, in zoos, sanctuaries, and other places.

Mitra wants to flood the traditional medicine market with those bones and carcasses. So do the owners of the 14 registered tiger farms in China. Mitra says prices will fall sharply if it happens. If prices fall far enough, tiger poachers will be undersold. If that happens, they'll stop killing tigers in the wild because they can't make money from it.

Mitra says the profits from the legal sales could help fund beefed-up anti-poaching programs, or nature programs that turn former poachers into park guards in the tiger's range. In other countries, these kinds of programs bring in millions every year.

"If even a fraction of that kind of money made its way to rural parts of India and China, you would see a sea change in attitudes" toward the wild tiger, says Mitra.

Mitra is the unofficial spokesman for the plan to save wild tigers by selling bones and organs from the tame ones. Recently, he toured some of China's tiger farms at the invitation of the Chinese government. China has no official position on the plan to open a market for farm-tiger parts, but conservationists and representatives of other governments say it's clear that the Chinese government likes the plan, as do the owners of the tiger farms.

Questions of Legitimacy

Most of China's tiger farms are open to the public. At the biggest farms, busloads of visitors drive around with big groups of tame tigers following behind. In others, according to Grace Gabriel of the International Fund for Animal Welfare, tourists pay to watch gangs of tigers shred cows dumped out of passing trucks.

Gabriel thinks these practices are inhumane and that the parks should be closed. She also worries that a legal trade in farmed tiger parts would lead to increased poaching, since there's no way to certify that a particular container of tiger-blood wine or powdered tiger bone came from a farmed animal.

Some believe that tigers may be saved from extinction through farms where they are treated humanely and sold for parts only after natural death occurs.

"It could come from wild tigers just as easily," Gabriel says. "It's going to make law enforcement (much) more difficult."

Gabriel doesn't think the owners of the tiger parks will agree to funnel any of the profits from these sales into beefed-up anti-poaching programs or into nature programs in the wild tiger's range. And she doesn't think the market-based plan to sell farmed tiger parts makes any economic sense.

That's a point that should be underlined, says economist Richard Damania of the University of Adelaide. He says there's no way a poacher who spends a maximum of $20 to kill a tiger will ever be undersold. Tiger farmers have to feed their animals from birth to death, which can costs thousands.

"That gap is so wide that it can never be closed," Damania said, "even if you factor in the cost of hunting down a tiger in the wild."

Wild and Captive Tiger Populations

There are almost as many tigers living on tiger farms as there are in the wild.

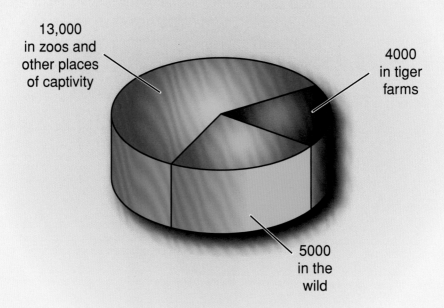

13,000 in zoos and other places of captivity

4000 in tiger farms

5000 in the wild

Taken from: Barun Mitra, National Public Radio; Sybille Klenzendorf, World Wildlife Fund; Brian Werner, Feline Conservation Federation

Farms Could Drive Up Demand

If anything, Damania says, the Mitra plan will lead to increased poaching by attracting a lot of buyers who would never think of purchasing anything on the black market. That would drive up demand, which would in turn drive up prices, he says. The incentive to poach would rise, and more wild tigers would be killed.

Damania says wild tigers living inside small preserves could be wiped out by poachers in a matter of years. Tigers living in bigger protected areas might manage to hang on, but not for very long.

"This new plan would be a death sentence," for the world's wild tigers, says Damania. But Barun Mitra of the Liberty Institute thinks those wild tigers may already be doomed, so why not gamble with the farming plan?

"I cannot understand how such an enormous and valuable economic asset can be left to rot" because of a ban on sales, he said, referring to the tiger carcasses he saw lined up in warehouses at some of the Chinese tiger farms.

One thing everyone involved in this debate agrees on is that poachers aren't the only threat facing the wild tigers of the world. For example, since the 1990s, nearly half of the lands the wild tigers used to live on have been cleared and occupied by people.

EVALUATING THE AUTHOR'S ARGUMENTS:

The author of this viewpoint describes the important role that tiger blood, bones, and organs play in traditional Asian medicines. These medicines are not well-known in North America, and it might be difficult for people living there to understand why they matter so much to people who live where the tigers live. In making decisions about protecting an endangered species like the tiger, how should people balance their love for a beautiful animal with their respect for another culture?

Tiger Farms Will Not Rescue Endangered Cats

Nirmal Ghosh

"Farming of critically endangered species has never saved them from extinction."

In the following viewpoint, Nirmal Ghosh argues that raising tigers on farms is not the way to protect them from extinction. While some people believe that raising tigers and selling parts of their bodies after they die would keep poachers from killing wild tigers for these same body parts, Ghosh contends that from an economic point of view, it will always be cheaper to kill tigers in the wild. He concludes that governments must take stronger steps to shut down illegal wildlife markets.

Ghosh is the Thailand correspondent for the leading South East Asian paper the *Straits Times*. He is a trustee of the Corbett Foundation, which works with communities near the Corbett Tiger Reserve in north India.

AS YOU READ, CONSIDER THE FOLLOWING QUESTIONS:

1. How many wild tigers are left in India, according to the viewpoint?
2. According to the author, how much does it cost to take care of one captive tiger for one year?
3. What evidence does the author give to show that tigers are popular with tourists?

Some people suggest that the only way to save some animals, like tigers, is to keep them in a zoo where breeding programs will save the species from extinction.

Asia has already permanently lost three of its original eight species of tigers. The rest, including those in India, are sliding rapidly towards extinction. The first to go will be the south China tiger, of which there are less than two dozen left in the wild.

It has become clear now that India has less than 2,000 tigers left in the wild across the entire country—fewer than the number of people that probably gather at any given weekday lunch hour between the Hindustan *Times* building on Kasturba Gandhi Marg [Road] and the Indian Oil building a block away.

It is by far the biggest population of all Asian countries but in historical terms a small one scattered in disparate groups, many marooned in isolated habitat and prone to inbreeding.

Protection in tiger habitats is often on paper, and corruption endemic not just in India but in many countries where they are found—making them fair game.

The Market for Tigers

A dead tiger can fetch up to US$ 40,000 in China, where the market is growing because of rising affluence. Tiger parts are used for a variety of purposes. Modern research in China itself has found tiger bones are not very different from dog and pig bones, but the appeal of the tiger is not based in reality, it is in the imagination of the consumer.

The global wildlife market, at around US$ 160 billion annually, is estimated to be the third largest in the world after arms and drugs, yet does not attract as much public attention as the first two.

A furious debate is now under way in the conservation community on how to save Asia's remaining wild tigers.

In the process an old idea has been revived—farming tigers to flood the market with their products, thereby driving prices down and reducing the incentive to poach. Revenue could even be used to fund conservation.

The problem is farming of critically endangered species has never saved them from extinction. For example, crocodiles are farmed in Thailand, but there are hardly any crocodiles left in the wild in that country.

Notes professor G. Agoramoorthy, a primatologist [someone who studies primates] teaching at Taiwan's Taipei University: "I have seen wildlife farms from South America to southeast Asia, all somehow directly or indirectly putting pressure on the existing wild populations of endangered species."

Debbie Banks of the London-based non-profit Environmental Investigation Agency, which has done extensive and definitive work on tigers, notes that traditional Chinese medicine is a global market

> **FAST FACT**
>
> In a one-week study, the International Fund for Animal Welfare found more than nine thousand live animals and products made from endangered species for sale on the Internet. One Web site offered two-week-old tiger cubs for fifteen hundred dollars each.

and the main reason for taking a tiger product is to inherit the animal's properties.

Indeed tiger part substitutes are available in China, but that has done nothing to dampen the demand for tiger products. In fact there is a "problem" with fake tiger products making money on this market.

Of eight tiger species, three have already become extinct, and the remaining five are endangered.

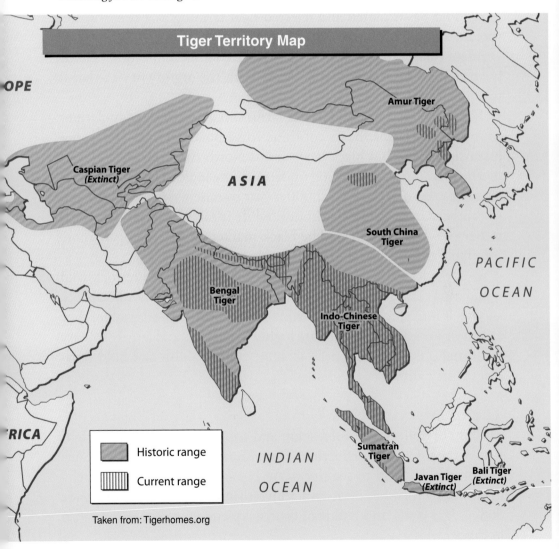

Tiger Territory Map

Taken from: Tigerhomes.org

Tigers and the Black Market

If farm tiger products were to be legalised, instead of currently banned worldwide under the Convention on International Trade in Endangered Species (CITES), a black market would quickly develop for the wild product. . . .

Opening the floodgates of this market for the tiger, would also fail to address the reasons why we have failed to protect it. Rather than fixing those problems, the solutions for which are known, those in favour of farming believe a new experiment will save the species.

"CITES has explored and rejected tiger farming as a conservation tool on a number of occasions," says Banks.

Adam Roberts of the US-based Born Free Foundation adds, "China instituted bear farming around 1984 with the argument . . . that it would reduce pressure on wild populations."

The exact opposite is true. Bear farms still deplete wild populations to stock their farms. Bears continue to be poached in the wild, not just Asiatic bears but black bears across North America.

The economics of poaching undermine the logic of free market balances; it takes around US$ 2,000 a year to raise a tiger to adulthood in captivity in passable conditions, while it takes around US$ 5–10 to have a wild tiger killed. The black market would be hugely more profitable than the farm product market.

Also, the logic that farm bred tigers could be used to restock wild populations is spurious. Farm-bred tigers would likely not be able to survive if introduced into the wild. Though they are adaptable, they are not American bison; they are highly specialised and largely solitary territorial predators who need to hunt, and establish and hold territory, to stay alive. . . .

The Charismatic Cats

Millions of dollars have been spent and scores of lives lost in the fight to save the tiger from extinction. Thousands of tourists flock to countries like India only to see tigers. At Thailand's infamous Sri Racha tiger farm, which has been under investigation by the authorities for dodgy tiger deals, thousands of tourists queue up to see bored tigers in cages.

Such is the drawing power of the giant cat. But unless governments seriously crack down on the illegal trade in wildlife, and sharpen protection of tiger habitat, the big cats will, in a tragic and irreversible irony, be hunted and eaten to extinction precisely because of their charisma. . . .

We cannot save our remaining tigers with an on-site protection system which is out of date. We need to fix what we have, not leave the status quo as it is and trying risky new experiments. If we cannot manage the basics, how are we going to manage a new set of problems?

EVALUATING THE AUTHOR'S ARGUMENTS:

The viewpoint you have just read spends a lot of time talking about money: How much it costs to raise a tiger in captivity and how much a dead tiger might sell for, for example. Why is it important to consider economic costs when making a plan to save an endangered species? How can planners decide how much is too much to spend to save these animals?

Chapter 3

Are the Needs of Humans More Important than Protecting Endangered Species?

Smoke from power plants could be polluting the air local wildlife needs to survive.

Drilling in the Arctic National Wildlife Refuge Will Endanger Wildlife

"This area is the most sensitive in the entire refuge and habitat loss that occurs here will impact the entire Arctic Refuge."

Defenders of Wildlife

In the following viewpoint, the authors argue that drilling for natural gas and oil in the Arctic National Wildlife Refuge would pose irreparable harm to the wildlife that live there. Polar bears, for example, make their dens and raise their young in the areas proposed for drilling, and because their dens are hard to see, they are hard to avoid. Other species, including migrating birds, would be threatened by interference with their habitat, the authors conclude.

Defenders of Wildlife, the creator of the Web site from which this viewpoint was taken, is a national conservation organization that works to protect native wild animals and plants in their natural communities.

AS YOU READ, CONSIDER THE FOLLOWING QUESTIONS:
1. What kinds of human actions are likely to disturb denning polar bears, according to the viewpoint?
2. According to the viewpoint, which two countries have worked together to protect the Porcupine Herd of caribou?
3. As reported by the authors, how many species of birds have been sighted in in the Arctic National Wildlife Refuge's coastal plain?

The Arctic National Wildlife Refuge, the largest wildlife refuge in the United States, encompasses 19 million acres and provides habitat to a diverse array of wildlife including millions of migratory birds, caribou, three species of bears (polar, grizzly and black bears), wolves, Dall sheep, muskoxen, arctic and red foxes, wolverines, plus many more. The nearby continental shelf provides the coastal waters with a rich nutrient base, which in turn supports a variety of marine mammals including the endangered bowhead whale.

The Arctic Refuge contains one of the most fragile and ecologically sensitive ecosystems in the world. It represents the only protected area in the world that includes an intact arctic, subarctic, and boreal ecosystem, thus retaining the natural dynamics that have existed for thousands of years. The Arctic environment is extremely vulnerable to long-lasting disturbance because the harsh climate and obviously short growing seasons allow species that have been harmed little time to recover.

The proposed oil and gas development would occur on the 1.5-million acre coastal plain found along the Beaufort Sea. This area is the most sensitive in the entire refuge and habitat loss that occurs here will impact the entire Arctic Refuge. The coastal plain habitat within the Arctic Refuge is also unique from other regions of the North Slope of Alaska because it is relatively narrow (only 15–40 miles across), limiting the alternatives for animals using these areas.

The following sections describe some of the species found on the coastal plain and how oil and gas development may adversely impact them. . . .

Some people are concerned that oil drilling operations in the Arctic National Wildlife Refuge could pose disastrous threats to the animals who live there.

Polar Bears

A symbol of the wild Arctic and an integral link in its complex food chain, proposals to drill for oil in the Arctic Refuge would have a huge impact on America's polar bear population. The coastal plain of the Arctic Refuge is the nation's most important onshore polar bear denning habitat. Pregnant females come ashore in November and December, build an ice den and give birth to one or two cubs. About 40% of the dens used by the Beaufort Sea population in Alaska are onshore and more than 60% of these are on the Arctic coastal plain.

Individual polar bear dens are extremely difficult to locate and therefore also difficult to avoid disturbing. Protection of onshore denning habitat is crucial because polar bears have a low rate of reproduction and are especially sensitive to human disturbances like aircraft, ships, road construction and traffic, pipelines, seismic work, drilling and oil transport activities. Once disturbed, polar bears may abandon their dens, leaving their cubs to die. According to a 1987 report by the U.S.

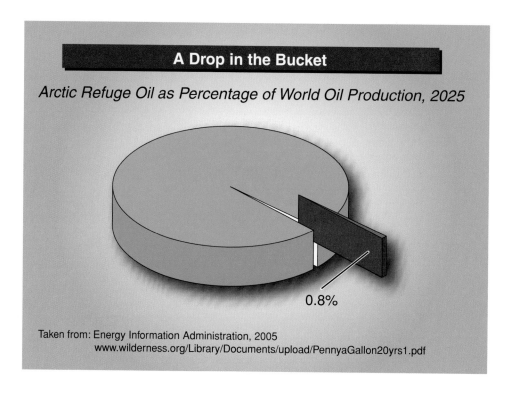

A Drop in the Bucket

Arctic Refuge Oil as Percentage of World Oil Production, 2025

0.8%

Taken from: Energy Information Administration, 2005
www.wilderness.org/Library/Documents/upload/PennyaGallon20yrs1.pdf

Fish and Wildlife Service, "early den abandonment can be fatal to cubs unable to fend for themselves or travel with their mother."

Oil spills can also be particularly catastrophic. The U.S. Fish and Wildlife Service (FWS) notes "Bears which have been fouled by oil may suffer thermo-regulatory problems, ingest oil, and may exhibit other detrimental effects such as inflammation of the nasal passages or central nervous system. Bears that contact oil are likely to die."

Because polar bears exist in relatively small populations and have low reproductive rates (only a quarter of the female bears become pregnant in any given year), they are highly susceptible to even small decreases in population numbers. Alaska's Beaufort Sea population of 1,800 polar bears appears to be stable currently, but even small decreases in bear cub survival or increases in female mortality could be devastating. . . .

Caribou

Two caribou herds, the Porcupine Herd and Central Arctic Herd, use the Arctic National Wildlife Refuge during one of the most critical periods of the year: to give birth and raise their young.

The Porcupine Herd is one of the largest caribou herds in North America numbering about 130,000 individuals. These animals manage to trudge through hundreds of miles of wilderness from south of the Brooks Range and across the Porcupine River in Canada's Yukon to drop their calves and feed on the nutritious plants of the Refuge's coastal plain. It's one of the planet's most magnificent wildlife migrations, second in distance only to the Wildebeests of Africa, and they've been doing it for tens of thousands of years.

In a treaty with Canada, the United States has agreed to protect this great herd. The herd's most heavily used calving area has been located within the coastal plain of the Arctic Refuge. This is the exact area that is proposed for drilling for oil. This is completely incompatible with the U.S. commitments to protect this herd.

The second herd also found within the coastal plain of the Arctic Refuge is the Central Arctic Herd. The Central Arctic Herd has achieved some notoriety as the caribou herd that has increased from 5,000 to about 27,000 while using the Prudhoe Bay oil fields. The truth is that many have been displaced away from oil development and those caribou that use the Arctic Refuge have better productivity than those displaced away from the Prudhoe Bay developments. This portion of the Central Arctic Herd also use the area designated as the 1002, for their calving and post-calving periods, a critical time for the successful rearing of their young. Development would also be expected to negatively influence the movements and reproductive success of this herd as well. . . .

Birds

Millions of migratory birds journey thousands of miles each spring to nest in the wetlands of the Arctic National Wildlife Refuge's coastal plain—the same area targeted for oil development by the oil industry, the [President George W.] Bush administration, and certain members of Congress. The birds travel from six continents and every state in the United States.

Over 135 species of waterfowl, shorebirds, songbirds, raptors and seabirds have been observed on the coastal plain of the Arctic Refuge. Oil drilling, with its associated roads, pipelines, processing plants, waste dumps, airstrips, and other industrial facilities would disturb these species' nesting and foraging habitats as well as potentially have toxic effects felt in the Arctic Refuge and wherever the birds travel. Of course, any declines of these migratory birds in Alaska would be felt on these birds' wintering grounds and migratory habitat in the rest of the country and beyond.

EVALUATING THE AUTHORS' ARGUMENTS:

Because drilling has not yet begun in the Arctic National Wildlife Refuge, arguments against such drilling are based on predictions. This means that in the viewpoint you have just read, the threats described to various animal species are threats that the authors believe will occur, not events that have already occurred. How does this affect your reading of the viewpoint? In deciding how to protect endangered species, how should the government decide whether to stop drilling before it starts or to allow drilling and wait to see whether it causes harm?

Drilling in the Arctic National Wildlife Refuge Will Not Harm Wildlife

Paul K. Driessen

"During eight months of winter, when drilling would take place, virtually no wildlife are present."

In the following viewpoint, Paul K. Driessen contends that drilling in the Arctic National Wildlife Refuge (ANWR) will provide much-needed oil and natural gas without threatening the wildlife that lives there. In fact, he argues, drilling in ANWR would actually threaten fewer animals than wind power, which some environmentalists prefer to the use of oil.

Driessen is a senior fellow with the Committee for a Constructive Tomorrow and the Center for the Defense of Free Enterprise, nonprofit public policy institutes that focus on energy, the environment, economic development, and international affairs. He is the author of *Eco-Imperialism: Green Power. Black Death* (2003).

AS YOU READ, CONSIDER THE FOLLOWING QUESTIONS:
1. As estimated by government geologists, how much oil could be recovered from the Arctic National Wildlife Refuge?
2. According to the viewpoint, why does Bat Conservation International oppose the increased use of wind power?
3. How do Inuit Eskimos living in the Arctic National Wildlife Refuge feel about the proposed drilling, according to the viewpoint?

The U.S. Senate budget bill would finally open the Arctic National Wildlife Refuge (ANWR) to drilling. Environmentalists are shocked and outraged. "This battle is far from over," they vowed.

Indeed, the 51–49 margin underscores the ideological passion of drilling opponents, their party-line determination to block [President George W.] Bush Administration initiatives, the misinformation that still surrounds this issue, and a monumental double standard for environmental protection.

FAST FACT

Including the 19 million acres in the Arctic National Wildlife Refuge, Alaska has 141 million acres of protected lands.

Many votes against drilling came from California and Northeastern senators who have made a career of railing against high energy prices, unemployment and balance of trade deficits—while simultaneously opposing oil and natural gas development in Alaska, the Outer Continental Shelf, western states and any other areas where petroleum might actually be found. Drilling in other countries is OK in their book, as is buying crude from oil-rich dictators, sending American jobs and dollars overseas, reducing US royalty and tax revenues, imperiling industries that depend on petroleum, and destroying habitats to generate "ecologically friendly" wind power.

This political theater of the absurd is bad enough. But many union bosses also oppose drilling, and thus kill jobs for their members—the epitome of hypocrisy.

A Lot of Oil in a Small Area

Government geologists say ANWR could hold up to 16 billion barrels of recoverable oil. That's 30 years' of imports from Saudi Arabia. Turned into gasoline, it would power California's vehicle fleet for 50 years, and hybrid and fuel cell cars would stretch the oil even further. ANWR's natural gas could fuel California's electrical generating plants for years.

Proposals call for only 2,000 acres to be developed in ANWR—a small portion of the total area.

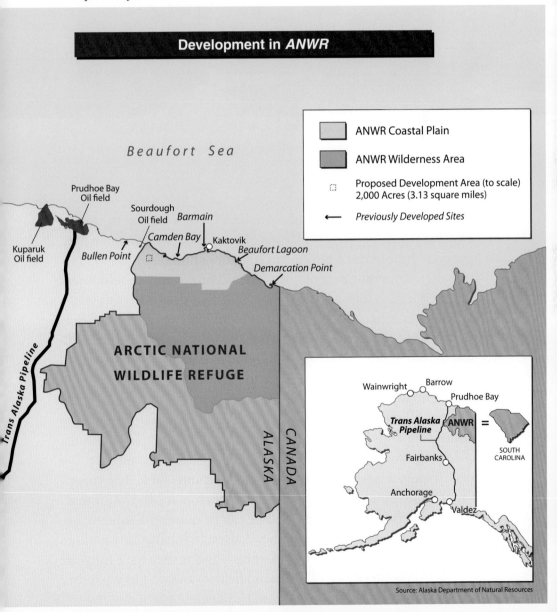

Development in *ANWR*

Beaufort Sea

ANWR Coastal Plain

ANWR Wilderness Area

Proposed Development Area (to scale)
2,000 Acres (3.13 square miles)

Previously Developed Sites

Prudhoe Bay Oil field

Sourdough Oil field

Barmain

Camden Bay

Kaktovik

Beaufort Lagoon

Kuparuk Oil field

Bullen Point

Demarcation Point

Trans Alaska Pipeline

ARCTIC NATIONAL WILDLIFE REFUGE

ALASKA

CANADA

Wainwright

Barrow

Prudhoe Bay

Trans Alaska Pipeline

ANWR

=

SOUTH CAROLINA

Fairbanks

Anchorage

Valdez

Source: Alaska Department of Natural Resources

Those who argue in favor of recovering oil from the Arctic National Wildlife Refuge believe that there are significant benefits to drilling, and that risks to wildlife who use the area can be minimized.

At $50 a barrel, ANWR could save the US from having to import $800 billion worth of foreign oil, create up to 700,000 American jobs, and generate hundreds of billions in royalties and taxes.

No matter, say environmentalists. They claim energy development would "irreparably destroy" the refuge. Caribou doo-doo.

ANWR is the size of South Carolina: 19 million acres. Of this, only 2,000 acres along the "coastal plain" would actually be disturbed by drilling and development. That's 0.01%—one-twentieth of Washington, DC—20 of the buildings Boeing uses to manufacture its 747 jets!

The potentially oil-rich area is a flat, treeless stretch of tundra, 3,500 miles from DC and 50 miles from the beautiful mountains seen in all the misleading anti-drilling photos. During eight months of winter, when drilling would take place, virtually no wildlife are present. No wonder. Winter temperatures drop as low as minus 40 F. The tundra turns rock solid. Spit, and your saliva freezes before it hits the ground.

But the nasty conditions mean drilling can be done with ice airstrips, roads and platforms. Come spring, they'd all melt, leaving only puddles and little holes. The caribou would return—just as they have for years at the nearby Prudhoe Bay and Alpine oil fields—and do just what they always have: eat, hang out and make babies. In fact, Prudhoe's caribou herd has increased from 6,000 head in 1978 to 27,000 today [2005]. Arctic fox, geese, shore birds and other wildlife would also return, along with the Alaska state bird, *Mosquito giganteus.*

Wind Power: A Dangerous Alternative

But the Wilderness Society, Sierra Club, Alaska Coalition, Defenders of Wildlife, and Natural Resources Defense Council still oppose ANWR development—even as they promote their favorite alternative to Arctic oil: wind energy. Electricity from wind is hardly a substitute for petroleum—especially for cars, trains, boats and planes. And swapping reliable, revenue-generating petroleum for intermittent, tax-subsidized wind power is a poor tradeoff.

On ecological grounds, wind power fails even more miserably.

A single 555-megawatt gas-fired power plant on 15 acres generates more electricity each year than do all 13,000 of California's wind turbines—which dominate 106,000 acres of once-scenic hill country. They kill some 10,000 eagles, hawks, other birds and bats every year.

On West Virginia's Backbone Mountain, 44 turbines killed numerous birds and 2,000 bats in 2003—and promoters want many more towers along this major migratory route over the Allegheny Front. But Conservation International and local politicians are livid.

In Wisconsin, anti-oil groups support building 133 gigantic Cuisinarts on 32,000 acres (16 times the ANWR operations area) near Horicon Marsh. This magnificent wetland is home to millions of geese, ducks and other migratory birds, and just miles from an abandoned mine that houses 140,000 bats. At 390 feet in height, the turbines tower over the Statue of Liberty (305 feet), US capitol (287 feet) and Arctic oil production facilities (50 feet).

All these turbines would produce about as much power as Fairfax County, Virginia gets from one facility that burns garbage to generate electricity. But they'd likely crank out an amazing amount of goose liver paté. . . .

A Threat to Native Residents?

The hypocrisy of this ecological double standard is palpable. So union bosses, greens and liberal politicians bring up the Gwich'in Indians, who claim drilling would "threaten their traditional lifestyle."

Inuit Eskimos who live in ANWR support drilling by an 8:1 margin. They're tired of living in poverty and using 5-gallon pails for toilets—after having given up their land claims for oil rights that Congress has repeatedly denied them.

The Gwich'ins live 150–250 miles away—and their reservations about drilling aren't exactly carved in stone. Back in the 1980s, the Alaska Gwich'ins leased 1.8 million acres of their tribal lands for oil development. That's more land than has been proposed for exploration in ANWR. (No oil was found.)

A couple years ago, Canada's Gwich'ins announced plans to drill in their 1.4-million-acre land claims area. The proposed drill sites (and a potential pipeline route) are just east of a major migratory path, where caribou often birth their calves, before they arrive in ANWR. . . .

Alternative energy technologies are certainly coming. Just ponder how we traveled, heated our homes, communicated and manufactured things 100 years ago—versus today. But the change won't happen overnight. Nor will it come via government mandates, or by throwing an anti-oil monkey wrench into our economy.

It shouldn't come at the expense of habitats, scenery and wildlife, either. Anyone who cares about these things should support automotive R&D [research and development]—and ANWR oil development.

EVALUATING THE AUTHOR'S ARGUMENTS:

The author of the viewpoint you have just read occasionally uses negative language to reinforce his arguments. He writes about the "double standard" and the "hypocrisy" of his opponents and refers to votes against drilling as a "political theater of the absurd." How does this kind of language affect the way you read the viewpoint? How can strong or negative language make an argument more forceful or less convincing?

Rain Forest Protection Programs Help Human Inhabitants

Jill Replogle

"[Forest concession is credited] with reducing deforestation, protecting watersheds and wet-land areas while provid-ing a steady income for local residents."

In the following viewpoint, Jill Replogle describes a program that protects rain forests in Guatemala by encouraging loggers to harvest trees responsibly. Unlike some rain forest inhabitants, who feel they must use up the trees in order to survive themselves, the residents of Guatemala's "concessions" benefit financially from the managed use of their trees. Replogle concludes that a coordinated effort to harvest trees wisely and to find customers willing to pay a premium for wood from these sustainable logging companies can bring much-needed income for the inhabitants while protecting the fragile rain forest.

Replogle, born in Arizona, lives in Guatemala and works as a correspondent for newspapers and radio.

Jill Replogle, "Village in Guatemalan Rain Forest Thrives with Ecological Logging," *San Francisco Chronicle*, August 22, 2005. Reproduced by permission of the author.

The loud drone of a gas generator and the buzz of power saws break the jungle silence. While a logger strips the bark off a mahogany tree, six teenage boys sand boards of Santa Maria, a popular hardwood used in furniture making.

Some of the finished product is destined for a college campus in the East Bay and a pool in San Francisco's Sunset District.

But unlike so much logging that has devastated forests throughout Latin America, including other areas of this 5 million acre rain forest in the Maya Biosphere Reserve, these workers toil under strict guidelines issued by a European organization that encourages responsible management of the world's forests. Many of their wood products are shipped to the United States and Europe.

"It's the best model in Latin America," said José Román Carrera, Central America forestry coordinator for the New York–based Rainforest Alliance.

Forest Concessions Support Local Families

The cooperative that works the 130,000-acre concession in the rain forest here consists of 56 impoverished families from the jungle village of Carmelita. It is one of 13 locally managed forest concessions the Guatemalan government has given to communities living in the reserve.

"We started by just selling mahogany logs and boards at the national level," said former cooperative president Juan Trujillo, who like other Carmelita residents once eked out a living collecting coagulated tree sap used to produce chewing gum. "Now we are trying to increase business" by selling processed wood abroad.

The concessions, which range from 125,000 acres to 200,000 acres, are logged in accordance with rules laid down by the Forest Stewardship Council, a nonprofit organization based in Bonn, Germany. Under the guidelines, only one or two trees per hectare (2.4 acres) can be extracted inside concession areas.

Forest Concessions Protect Habitats

Environmental organizations credit the approach with reducing defor-estation, protecting watersheds and wetland areas while providing a steady income for local residents.

"The best preserved places in the reserve are in the concession areas," said Liza Grandia, a UC [University of California] Berkeley anthropologist who has worked with Carmelita and other reserve com-munities. "They have done an incredible job, even though many have only a third-grade education."

Scientists predict that as population increases, the world's rainforests will continue to be consumed at an increasingly accelerating rate.

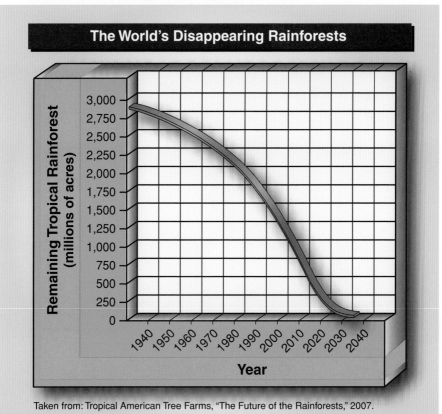

Taken from: Tropical American Tree Farms, "The Future of the Rainforests," 2007.

The Maya Biosphere Reserve is Central America's most biologically diverse rain forest, one of the largest jungle areas north of the Amazon. It is home to such endangered species as jaguar and scarlet macaw and more than 200 Mayan archaeological sites.

Although 36 percent of the reserve is protected by law, some of its most prominent national parks have suffered major destruction in recent years due to illegal settlers, ranchers, poachers and drug traffickers. More than half of Laguna del Tigre National Park, a vast wetland area, has been burned for ranching and farming in the past several years, environmentalists say.

Yet recent satellite photos by the U.S. Geological Survey show forest coverage remains mostly intact in the area under concession to 11 communities and two timber companies.

Catering to the Green Building Movement

To be sure, these rain forest communities are taking advantage of the rapidly expanding green building movement in the United States and increased demand for certified wood.

According to some, introducing sustainable logging practices in South America can prevent rapid deforestation while providing stable income for local communities.

Last year [2004], California Gov. Arnold Schwarzenegger signed an executive order requiring all new or renovated state-owned facilities to be certified by the Leadership in Energy and Environmental Design (LEED) program created by the U.S. Green Building Council. LEED rates facilities on a range of eco-friendly standards, including energy and water efficiency, and the use of environmentally sound building resources, including certified wood.

Robin Bass, a member of LEED's steering committee for Northern California, says an increasing number of private companies have pledged to meet the group's eco-standards. "It's good for business . . . great for your bottom line," she said.

In June [2005], San Francisco became the first U.S. city to enact a law that requires city departments to buy products that do as little harm as possible to people and the earth. More recently, Mayor Gavin Newsom announced the city had become the nation's first to apply high environmental standards to all its new affordable housing developments, including the use of solar panels and recycled building materials.

San Francisco architects also say they plan to use wood certified by the Forest Stewardship Council from the Maya Biosphere Reserve for a construction project at Sava Pool in the Sunset District, and similarly certified wood from Brazil to be fashioned into benches near the new de Young Museum in Golden Gate Park. But Mark Palmer, the green building coordinator for San Francisco's Department of the Environment, says both projects are on hold until city regulations can be modified. In the early 1990s, San Francisco barred tropical hardwood because of unfettered logging. Palmer says a public hearing on approving certified wood is scheduled for next month [September 2005].

"We want to encourage well-managed forest practices, and this is the way we can do it, through purchasing practices," Palmer said.

FAST FACT

Harry Potter and the Half-Blood Prince was the first best-selling book published in the United Kingdom printed on paper made only from forests certified as "well managed" by the Forest Stewardship Council.

Early this year, Oakland's EarthSource Forest Products bought 300,000 board feet of mahogany and 600,000 board feet of lesser-known tropical hardwoods from the reserve. The East Bay company supplies such Bay Area firms as San Francisco's MBT Architecture, which is using a reddish Guatemalan hardwood known as machiche in the construction of Ohlone College's new satellite campus in Newark, according to MBT architect Susan Seastone.

A Future of Possibilities

Meanwhile, eight reserve communities—including Carmelita—are hoping to increase their income with recently opened sawmills financed partly by Rainforest Alliance and the U.S. Agency for International Development.

Although logging has brought Carmelita running water and a new primary school, villagers hope the new venture will soon bring them electricity and other advances.

"There is now more work and more possibilities for our children," said Ana Centeno, a member of the Carmelita cooperative.

EVALUATING THE AUTHOR'S ARGUMENTS:

Why does the author of the viewpoint you have just read devote so much attention to the customers in the United States and other countries who purchase wood? What is the role that people in large cities like San Francisco play in protecting endangered species in rain forests, wilderness areas, and other fragile habitats far away?

Rain Forest Protection Programs Harm Human Inhabitants

"Activities of conservation organizations now represent the single biggest threat to the integrity of indigenous lands."

Mark Dowie

In the following viewpoint, Mark Dowie describes the plight of native residents of several areas of the world that have been identified as habitats for endangered species. Many of these inhabitants, he argues, have been forcibly and unjustly removed from their homes with little regard for their wishes or their well-being. He concludes that the best way to preserve biological diversity is to leave fragile habitats in the care of the indigenous residents, who have already developed sustainable ways to live in them.

Dowie teaches science at the University of California Berkeley Graduate School of Journalism. His work has won four National Magazine Awards.

Mark Dowie, "Conservation Refugees," *Orion*, November-December, 2005, pp. 16-27. Copyright © 2005 The Orion Society. Reproduced by permission of the author.

AS YOU READ, CONSIDER THE FOLLOWING QUESTIONS:
1. What controversy resulted in the Batwa people being evicted from their homeland in Uganda, according to the viewpoint?
2. As explained by the Maasai leader Martin Saning'o, why are traditional Maasai farming techniques good for the environment?
3. As the viewpoint explains, how are conservation refugees different from economic refugees?

A low fog envelops the steep and remote valleys of southwestern Uganda most mornings, as birds found only in this small corner of the continent rise in chorus and the great apes drink from clear streams. Days in the dense montane forest are quiet and steamy. Nights are an exaltation of insects and primate howling. For thousands of years the Batwa people thrived in this soundscape, in such close harmony with the forest that early-twentieth-century wildlife biologists who studied the flora and fauna of the region barely notice their existence. They were, as one naturalist noted, "part of the fauna."

In the 1930s, Ugandan leaders were persuaded by international conservationists that this area was threatened by loggers, miners, and other extractive interests. In response, three forest reserves were created—the Mgahinga, the Echuya, and the Bwindi—all of which overlapped with the Batwa's ancestral territory. For sixty years these reserves simply existed on paper, which kept them off-limits to extractors. And the Batwa stayed on, living as they had for generations, in reciprocity with the diverse biota that first drew conservationists to the region.

FAST FACT

Approximately 50 million native people live in the world's rainforests, according to the Rainforest Foundation.

However, when the reserves were formally designated as national parks in 1991 and a bureaucracy was created and funded by the World Bank's Global Environment Facility to manage them, a rumor was in circulation that the Batwa were hunting and eating silverback gorillas, which by that time where widely recognized as a threatened species and also, increasingly, as a featured attraction for ecotourists from Europe and America. Gorillas were being disturbed and even poached, the Batwa admitted, but by Bahutu, Batutsi, Bantu, and other tribes who invaded the forest from outside villages. The Batwa, who felt a strong kinship with the great apes, adamantly denied killing them. Nonetheless, under pressure from traditional Western conservationists, who had come to believe that wilderness and human community were incompatible, the Batwa were forcibly expelled from their homeland.

These forests are so dense that the Batwa lost perspective when they first came out. Some even stepped in front of moving vehicles. Now they are living in shabby squatter camps on the perimeter of the parks, without running water or sanitation. . . .

In one more generation their forest-based culture—songs, rituals, traditions, and stories—will be gone.

Conservation Refugees

It's no secret that millions of native peoples around the world have been pushed off their land to make room for big oil, big metal, big timber, and big agriculture. But few people realize that the same thing has happened for a much nobler cause: land and wildlife conservation. . . .

In early 2004 a United Nations [UN] meeting was convened in New York for the ninth year in a row to push for passage of a resolution protecting the territorial and human rights of indigenous peoples. The UN draft declaration states: "Indigenous peoples shall not be forcibly removed from their lands or territories. No relocation shall take place without the free and informed consent of the indigenous peoples concerned and after agreement on just and fair compensation and, where possible, with the option to return." During the meeting an indigenous delegate who did not identify herself rose to state that while extractive industries were still a serious threat to their welfare and cultural integrity, their new and biggest enemy was "conservation."

Later that spring, at a Vancouver, British Columbia, meeting of the International Forum on Indigenous Mapping, all two hundred delegates signed a declaration stating that the "activities of conservation organizations now represent the single biggest threat to the integrity of indigenous lands." . . .

Conservation efforts in Africa have displaced many of the human inhabitants of those lands.

"We are enemies of conservation," declared Maasai leader Martin Saning'o, standing before a session of the November 2004 World Conservation Congress sponsored by IUCN [World Conservation Union] in Bangkok, Thailand. The nomadic Maasai, who have over the past thirty years lost most of their grazing range to conservation projects throughout eastern Africa, hadn't always felt that way. In fact, Saning'o reminded his audience, "we were the original conservationists." The room was hushed as he quietly explained how pastoral and nomadic cattlemen have traditionally protected their range: "Our ways of farming pollinated diverse seed species and maintained corridors between ecosystems." Then he tried to fathom the strange version of land conservation that has impoverished his people, more than one hundred thousand of whom have been displaced from southern Kenya and the Serengeti Plains of Tanzania. Like the Batwa, the Maasai have not been fairly compensated. Their culture is dissolving and they live in poverty.

"We don't want to be like you," Saning'o told a room of shocked white faces. "We want you to be like us. We are here to change your minds. You cannot accomplish conservation without us."

A Worldwide Movement

Although he might not have realized it, Saning'o was speaking for a growing worldwide movement of indigenous peoples who think of themselves as conservation refugees. Not to be confused with ecological refugees—people forced to abandon their homelands as a result of unbeatable heat, drought, desert, desertification, flooding, disease, or other consequences of climate chaos—conservation refugees are removed from their lands involuntarily, either forcibly or through a variety of less coercive measures. The gentler, more benign methods are sometimes called "soft eviction" or "voluntary resettlement," though the latter is contestable. . . .

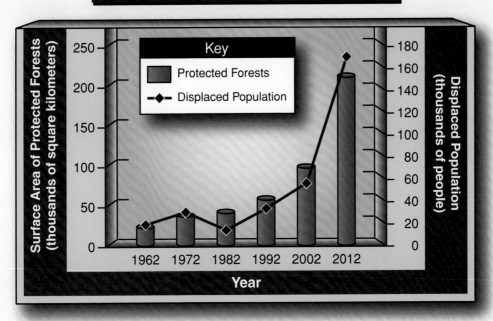

The Surface Area of Protected Areas and the Number of Displaced People

Taken from: Michael M. Cernea and Kai Schmidt-Soltau. Biodiversity Conservation versus Population Resettlement. Paper presented at the International Conference on Rural Livelihoods, Forests and Biodiversity. 19–23 May 2003.

Indigenous peoples are often left out of the process entirely.

More and more conservationists seem to be wondering how, after setting aside a "protected" landmass the size of Africa, global biodiversity continues to decline. Might there be something terribly wrong with this plan—particularly after the Convention on Biological Diversity has documented the astounding fact that in Africa, where so many parks and reserves have been created and where indigenous evictions run highest, 90 percent of biodiversity lies outside of protected areas? If we want to preserve biodiversity in the far reaches of the globe, places that are in many cases still occupied by indigenous people living in ways that are ecologically sustainable, history is showing us that the dumbest thing we can do is kick them out.

EVALUATING THE AUTHOR'S ARGUMENTS:

Several of the viewpoints in this book, including the one you have just read, deal with conflicts between protecting endangered species and the needs and rights of humans who live near them. How should governments decide when it is best to limit the rights of humans in order to protect plants and animals? What steps could be taken to help humans who are affected by these decisions feel better about their losses?

Viewpoint 5

The Military Should Restrict the Use of Sonar to Protect Endangered Whales

"The Navy's active sonar program appears to be responsible for many more whale strandings than had previously been imagined."

Natural Resources Defense Council

In the following viewpoint, the Natural Resources Defense Council argues that sonar systems, used by the U.S. Navy and the militaries of other countries to detect enemy submarines, harm endangered whales and other marine mammals. The Council contends that scientists have demonstrated that several instances of whales dying on the world's beaches can be directly traced to military use of sonar. The Council concludes that the Navy could protect whales by making reasonable reductions in the scope of its sonar programs.

Founded in 1970, the Natural Resources Defense Council, with more than one million members, is an environmental action organization that works to protect wildlife and its habitat.

AS YOU READ, CONSIDER THE FOLLOWING QUESTIONS:
1. According to the viewpoint, how could the Navy ensure that whales and other mammals are not present in the area before turning on its active sonar?
2. Why do researchers think the population of Cuvier's beaked whales that used to inhabit the waters near the Bahaman Islands has disappeared, according to the viewpoint?
3. As described by the Natural Resources Defense Council, what are some of the ways that whales use sound?

According to a report by the scientific committee of the International Whaling Commission, one of the world's leading bodies of whale biologists, the evidence linking sonar to a series of whale strandings in recent years is "very convincing and appears overwhelming." Despite the broad scientific consensus that military active sonar kills whales, the use of this deadly sonar in the world's oceans is spreading.

An NRDC [National Resources Defense Council]-led coalition of wildlife advocates succeeded in restricting the U.S. Navy's use of a powerful active sonar system known as SURTASS LFA [Surveillance Towed Array Sensor System Low Frequency Active] in 2003. But the fight is hardly over; other nations are developing LFA-type systems of their own, and sonar testing using mid-frequency sonar systems, which have been implicated in numerous strandings of whales worldwide, continues unabated, putting marine mammals and fisheries at risk. . . .

In response, NRDC and its partners have redoubled our campaign, both at home and abroad, to control the spread of this harmful technology. In October 2005, after attempting for years to engage the Navy in constructive dialogue on the harms caused by its mid-frequency sonar systems, NRDC brought suit in U.S. federal court, together with a coalition of wildlife advocates, asking that the Navy take common-sense precautions during peacetime training with mid-frequency sonar.

Such measures include, for example, putting rich marine mammal habitat off limits; avoiding migration routes and feeding or breeding areas when marine mammals are present; and listening with passive sonar to ensure marine mammals are not in the testing area before switching on active sonar. . . .

Active Sonar: How It Harms Marine Life

Military active sonar works like a floodlight, emitting sound waves that sweep across tens or even hundreds of miles of ocean, revealing objects in their path. But that kind of power requires the use of extremely loud sound. Each loudspeaker in the LFA system's wide array, for example, can generate 215 decibels' worth—sound as intense as that produced by a twin-engine fighter jet at takeoff. Some mid-frequency sonar systems can put out over 235 decibels, as loud as a Saturn V rocket at launch. Even 100 miles from the LFA system, sound levels can approach 160 decibels, well beyond the Navy's own safety limits for humans.

Evidence of the harm such a barrage of sound can do began to surface in March 2000, when whales of four different species stranded themselves on beaches in the Bahamas after a U.S. Navy battle group used active sonar in the area. Investigators found that the whales were bleeding internally around their brains and ears. Although the Navy initially denied responsibility, the government's investigation

Some believe that military use of sonar is contributing to a decrease in marine life populations for species like whales.

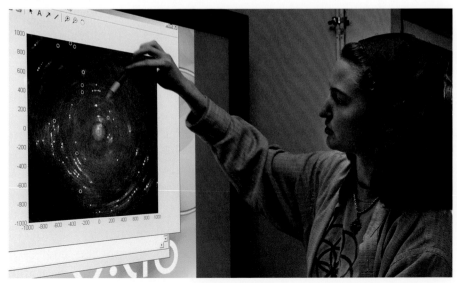

established with virtual certainty that the strandings were caused by its use of active sonar. Since the incident, the area's population of Cuvier's beaked whales has all but disappeared, leading researchers to conclude that they either abandoned their habitat or died at sea.

The Bahamas, it turned out, was only the tip of an iceberg. Additional mass strandings and deaths associated with military activities and active sonar have occurred in Madeira (2000), Greece (1996), the U.S. Virgin Islands (1998, 1999), the Canary Islands (1985, 1988, 1989, 2002, 2004), the northwest coast of the United States (2003) and coastal waters off North Carolina (2005). And in July 2004 researchers uncovered an extraordinary concentration of whale strandings near Yokosuka, a major U.S. Navy base off the Pacific coast of Japan. The Navy's active sonar program appears to be responsible for many more whale strandings than had previously been imagined.

> ## FAST FACT
>
> The humpback whale is one of the most endangered of the large whales. Scientists estimate that there are between two thousand and four thousand remaining in the western North Atlantic.

How does active sonar harm whales? According to a report in the scientific journal *Nature*, animals that came ashore during one mass stranding had developed large emboli, or bubbles, in their organ tissue. The report suggested that the animals had suffered from something akin to a severe case of "the bends"—the illness that can kill scuba divers who surface too quickly from deep water. The study supports what many scientists have long suspected: that the whales stranded on shore are only the most visible symptom of a problem affecting much larger numbers of marine life.

Other impacts, though more subtle, are no less serious. Marine mammals and many species of fish use sound to follow migratory routes, locate each other over great distances, find food and care for their young. Noise that undermines their ability to hear can threaten their ability to function and, over the long term, to survive. Naval sonar has been shown to alter the singing of humpback whales, an activity essential to the reproduction of this endangered species; to disrupt the feeding of orcas; and to cause porpoises and other species to leap from the water,

How Loud Is Sonar?

A comparison of sound volumes in air and in water shows that a sonar signal that reaches a whale at 150 decibels sounds as loud to the whale as a jackhammer is to humans.

(Decibels in air)

150	
140	
130	Jet engine
120	
110	Live rock music
100	
90	Jackhammer
80	
70	
60	Normal conversation
50	
40	

(Decibels in water)

Supertankers	210
	200
Level of whale communication	190
	180
General shipping noise	170
	160
	150
	140
	130
Behavior changes seen in 50% of gray whales	120
	110
	100

Key

Humans on land   Whales in ocean

Taken from: Illustration from Rod Thompson, "The Sound and the Fury," *Honolulu Star Bulletin*, March 12, 1998

or panic and flee. Over time, these effects could undermine the fitness of populations of animals, contributing to what prominent biologist Sylvia Earle has called "a death of a thousand cuts."

Reining in LFA Sonar

Since 1994, when NRDC began investigating rumors that sound experiments were taking place off the California coast, LFA (Low-Frequency Active) sonar has been of particular concern because of the enormous distances traveled by its intense blasts of sound. During testing off the California coast, noise from a single LFA system was detected across the breadth of the North Pacific. By the Navy's own estimates, even 300 miles from the source these sonic waves can retain an intensity of 140 decibels— still a hundred times more intense than the noise aversion threshold for gray whales. Many scientists believe that blanketing the oceans with such deafening sound could harm entire populations of whales, dolphins and fish.

NRDC's decade-long campaign to expose the dangers of active sonar won a major victory in August 2003, when a federal court ruled illegal the Navy's plan to deploy LFA sonar through 75 percent of the world's oceans. On the heels of this ruling, the Navy agreed to limit use of the system to a fraction of the area originally proposed, and that use of LFA sonar will be guided by negotiated geographical limits and seasonal exclusions. Conservationists believe this will protect critical habitat and whale migrations, and the Navy also retains the flexibility it needs for training exercises. None of the limits apply during war or heightened threat conditions. The pact demonstrates that current law can safeguard both the environment and national security.

But the ink was barely dry on the historic settlement when the [President George W.] Bush administration pushed legislation through Congress that exempts the U.S. military from core provisions of the Marine Mammal Protection Act—leaving the armed forces much freer to harm whales, dolphins and other marine mammals in the course of using high-intensity sonar and underwater explosives. Exemptions in hand, the administration is now appealing the ruling limiting deployment of LFA sonar—a hard-won court victory NRDC stands ready to defend.

EVALUATING THE AUTHOR'S ARGUMENTS:

The viewpoint you have just read emphasizes the harm caused by sonar, but does not spend much time describing the benefits of using sonar. The next viewpoint, "The Military Need Not Restrict the Use of Sonar to Protect Endangered Whales," emphasizes the reasons for operating sonar systems, but does not spend much time describing the drawbacks. How should citizens go about making good decisions when presented with limited information? What questions might you ask the authors of both viewpoints in order to feel satisfied that you understood the issues thoroughly?

The Military Need Not Restrict the Use of Sonar to Protect Endangered Whales

"Sonar has been linked with only a very small fraction of marine mammal strandings worldwide."

United States Navy

In the following viewpoint, writers representing the U.S. Navy argue that the use of sonar to detect enemy submarines is increasingly important in today's world. The authors describe steps the Navy has taken to study the effects of sonar on whales and other marine mammals and argue that the Navy takes reasonable precautions to avoid harming them. They conclude, however, that the Navy's primary responsibility is to defend the nation, not to protect animals.

The U.S. Navy operates low frequency active (LFA) sonar systems in oceans around the world.

United States Navy: Defending the Nation, Protecting the Environment, n.d. <www.whalesandsonar.navy.mil>

AS YOU READ, CONSIDER THE FOLLOWING QUESTIONS:
1. According to the authors, what two responsibilities must the U.S. Navy balance in determining how to use sonar?
2. As described by the viewpoint, what sounds might be heard in the ocean, in addition to the sounds whales and other mammals make?
3. What does the term *stranding* mean in the context of this viewpoint?

Sonar is an invaluable tool for protecting our nation. Its importance has grown in recent years as more and more nations have acquired inexpensive, very quiet submarines. Sonar is the only effective means we have to detect and quickly target hostile submarines and keep sea lanes open for commercial ships and oil tankers, as well as our naval forces. Our sonar operators must receive real-life training and experience at sea in order to protect our nation's ships, shores, and allies.

As responsible environmental stewards, the U.S. Navy is concerned about the potential effects of active sonar on marine mammals and is committed to complying with all applicable federal laws, regulation and policies. The Navy spends millions of dollars each year on marine mammal research to better understand the potential effects of manmade sound on marine mammals to help ensure that Navy policy and compliance are based on real science.

The U.S. Navy will continue to seek solutions that are protective of marine life while maintaining warfighting proficiency and crew safety. We will continue our active participation in appropriate forums and will respond to incidents involving marine life on the basis of sound science and factual inquiry. We are committed to maintaining the balance between defending freedom and remaining good stewards of the environment.

Marine Mammals and Sound

All pinnipeds and cetaceans depend on sound to some degree to sense the ocean environment, and some are known to use echolocation. Echolocation allows these animals to determine the distance of objects (food, predators) and features of the underwater environment

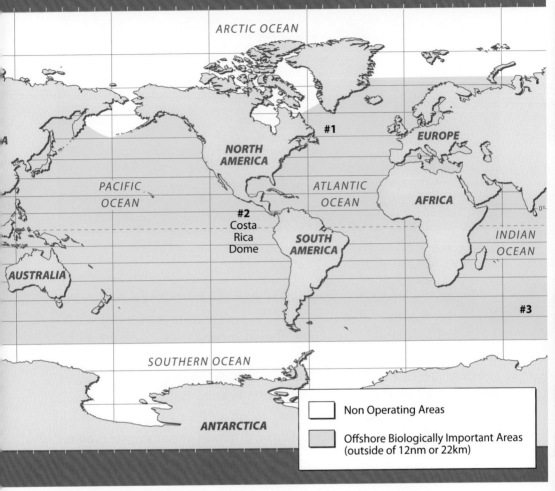

ARCTIC OCEAN

#1

EUROPE

NORTH
AMERICA

PACIFIC
OCEAN

ATLANTIC
OCEAN

AFRICA

#2
Costa
Rica
Dome

SOUTH
AMERICA

INDIAN
OCEAN

AUSTRALIA

#3

SOUTHERN OCEAN

ANTARCTICA

Non Operating Areas

Offshore Biologically Important Areas
(outside of 12nm or 22km)

*The Navy will avoid biologically sensitive areas when deploying its Surveillance
Towed Array Sensor System Low Frequency Active (SURTASS LFA) Sonar.*

(seafloor depth, topography) for navigation purposes. They accomplish this by projecting sounds, called sonar clicks, that are reflected back when the sounds strike an object The farther away an object is, the longer it takes for the echo to return, allowing the echolocating animal to tell the distance. Echolocation makes it possible to navigate and feed at night and in deep or murky water, or at great distances where visual sensing would be ineffective. For example, a dolphin can detect a target the size of a golf ball almost a football field away, much farther than the dolphin can see underwater.

According to U.S. Navy sources, maneuvers with sonar may not pose a serious threat to marine wildlife.

Marine mammals also use underwater vocalizations to communicate with each other. Because sound waves travel efficiently in water, some ocean-dwelling animals are able to communicate over great distances through sound. . . .

There are 119 species of marine mammals, ranging from one to 40 meters in length and from 45 to 95,000 kg [kilograms] in mass. These species have widely varying sensitivities to sound based on frequency. This is a reflection of how different species have evolved to cope with life in the marine environment, including differences in size, prey, habitats, and the predators they try to avoid. Species that live in the same habitat may have overlapping, but not necessarily identical, hearing ranges. . . .

The ocean is inherently a noisy environment. Seismic disturbances, snapping shrimp and sounds from other ocean dwellers, rain, lightning strikes, and of course manmade sounds such as offshore drilling, seismic surveys, commercial shipping and other ship sounds, fishing boats, recreational boating, and sonar use contribute to the background sound in today's oceans.

Years of research and a significant investment on the part of the U.S. Navy and other organizations have shed light on the hearing abilities of only a limited number of marine mammal species. It is clear that mankind knows relatively little about how the majority of marine mammals hear and how they may be affected by sound. The National Academy of Sciences has recommended that research be conducted to detect subtle changes in marine mammal behavior that could result from manmade sound interfering with biologically important acoustic information. Short-term responses of marine mammals to anthropogenic sound have been documented to a limited degree. Research to date has shown that marine mammals react to manmade sound in some cases, but do not react in other cases.

The Navy is concerned about the potential effects of active sonar on marine mammals, and funds research annually to better understand how marine mammals hear and how they may be affected by manmade sound. At the same time, the Navy's Title 10 responsibilities under the U.S. Code require us to be prepared for combat at sea to defend the United States, and these responsibilities cannot be met without active sonar and the real-life training required to use it. Based on the technology available today, active sonar is the only effective means for the men and women aboard ship to defend against hostile submarine threats. The Navy will continue to fund research and use mitigation measures to minimize the potential effects of sonar on marine mammals, but cannot put the lives of its Sailors at risk or fail to remain prepared to defend our nation by eliminating active sonar use.

Stranding Events

According to the National Marine Fisheries Service (NOAA Fisheries), strandings occur when marine mammals or sea turtles swim or float into shore and become beached or stuck in shallow water. Strandings have occurred for hundreds of years and in many parts of the world. According to NOAA Fisheries, in 1999 alone, more than 3,000 marine mammals stranded on U.S. shores. In the five years from 1994 through 1998, 19,130 strandings were reported, an average of 3,826 per year.

In most cases, the cause of strandings is unknown, but some identified causes include disease, parasite infestation, harmful algal blooms, injuries from ship strikes

FAST FACT

In 2006 there were 244 submarines operated by countries that are not allied with the United States, according to the U.S. Navy.

or fishery entanglements, exposure to pollution, trauma, and starvation. Strandings also occur after unusual weather or oceanographic events.

Sonar has been linked with only a very small fraction of marine mammal strandings worldwide. One incident, in which several whales stranded in the Bahamas in March of 2000 following a chokepoint exercise, was a confluence of several factors acting together including numbers of sonars, unusual bathymetry, limited egress routes, and specific species of marine mammal. As a result of this incident, the Navy avoids training in coastal areas with bathymetry similar to the Bahamas when possible, and also avoids other known beaked whale concentration areas.

The Navy and NOAA Fisheries learned from the Bahamas stranding that certain marine mammals, particularly beaked whales, may be sensitive to mid-frequency sonar. The Navy is concerned about the potential for sonar to negatively affect marine mammals, and is working with ocean agencies, academic institutions and independent researchers around the world to better understand what combinations of ocean conditions, geography, and sonar use may lead to marine mammal disturbances.

Historical records show that marine-mammal strandings have taken place for centuries, well before the advent of sonar. Nonetheless, the Navy remains dedicated to improving the collective understanding of the effects of sonar on marine mammals and to minimizing adverse effects of sonar consistent with our responsibility to defend the nation and ensure the safety of our Sailors, Airmen and Marines. For this purpose, the Navy funds scientific research and implements protective measures as needed to minimize the potential for effects on marine mammals.

EVALUATING THE AUTHOR'S ARGUMENTS:

The viewpoint you have just read begins and ends with a reminder that the U.S. Navy is charged with national defense and with the safety of its servicemen and servicewomen. How does this reminder affect the way you read the viewpoint? Do you accept the authors' arguments? Explain your answer.

Facts About Endangered Species

Endangered Species in the United States

As of April 2007, the U.S. Fish and Wildlife Service reports:

- There are 1,312 species in the United States that are threatened or endangered: 568 animals and 744 plants.
- Twelve mammal species are listed as threatened, and seventy are listed as endangered.
- Fifteen bird species are threatened, and seventy-six species are endangered.
- Sixty-four fish species are threatened, and seventy-four species are endangered.
- The largest group of threatened and endangered species in the United States is flowering plants. There are 143 species of flowering plants that are considered threatened, while 570 species are considered endangered.

The U.S. Fish and Wildlife Service reported at the end of 2005:

- The states with the highest numbers of threatened and endangered species are Hawaii (312 species), Arizona (295), Florida (101), and Alabama (89).
- The states with the fewest threatened and endangered species are Washington, D.C. (3), North Dakota (7), Alaska (8), Vermont (8), and Rhode Island (9).

According to Defenders of Wildlife, grizzly bears have the following characteristics:

- The Latin name for the grizzly bear—also called the brown bear—is *Ursus arctos horribilis.*
- Adult males weigh from 300 to 850 pounds, while females weigh between 200 and 450 pounds. The largest bears are found along the coasts of Alaska and British Columbia, where salmon is plentiful.
- Grizzlies can move quickly, running as fast as 35–40 miles per hour.

- While there are only approximately one thousand grizzly bears in the lower forty-eight states, there are more than thirty thousand in Alaska.
- Grizzlies live approximately thirty years in the wild, but can live for fifty years in zoos.
- Grizzly cubs stay with their mothers for two to four years, and females will not bear another litter until one family of cubs is old enough to live independently.

Endangered Species Around the World

According to the World Conservation Union's 2006 Red List of threatened species:

- There are 5,624 threatened vertebrate species: 1,206 bird species, 1,811 amphibian species, 1,173 fish species, 1,093 mammal species, and 341 reptile species.
- There are 2,101 threatened invertebrate species, including insects, mollusks, crustaceans, and others.
- There are 8,390 threatened plant species.
- There are three threatened lichen and mushroom species.

Greenpeace International reports the following about threatened and endangered whales:

- The blue whale, considered to be endangered but slowly recovering, is the largest animal that has ever lived on earth, larger even than the dinosaurs. A blue whale can reach 108 feet in length and weigh as much as 240,000 pounds.
- The grey whale, also considered endangered but slowly recovering, migrates every year from the west coast of Mexico, where baby whales are born, up the west coast of the United States and Canada to the Bering Sea, where the whales feed in winter. The total round trip every year is 2,200 to 3,800 miles.
- The humpback whale, considered endangered and heading toward extinction, is famous for its underwater communications called "songs." These songs are longer and more complex than those of any other animal.

Defenders of Wildlife reports the following about tigers:

- The Latin name for the tiger is *Panthera tigris*.

- The tiger is the largest member of the cat species.
- Five tiger subspecies still live on earth: Bengal, Chinese, Indochinese, Siberian, and Sumatran tigers. Three subspecies—Bali, Caspian, and Javan—are extinct.
- Tigers can reach up to ten feet long from nose to tail and weigh up to 400 to 575 pounds.
- Tigers live ten to fifteen years in the wild.

According to the Rainforest Protection Network:
- Tropical rainforests are home to more than 50 percent of the Earth's species.
- A typical four-square-mile patch of tropical rainforest contains up to 1,500 flowering plants species, 750 tree species, 125 mammal species, 400 bird species, 100 reptile species, 60 amphibian species, and 150 butterfly species.

The World Resources Institute reports:
- One hundred species become extinct every day due to the loss of tropical rainforests.
- Unless dramatic steps are taken to change the present course, approximately 5 to 10 percent of tropical forest species could become extinct each decade during the next half-century.

National Surveys About Endangered Species and the Environment

According to a March 2006 Gallup Poll:
- Thirty-four percent of people worry a "great deal" about the extinction of plant and animal species, while 29 percent worry a "fair amount," 23 percent worry "only a little," and 14 percent worry "not at all."
- Asked about the loss of tropical rain forests, 40 percent worry a "great deal," 24 percent worry a "fair amount," 22 percent worry "only a little," and 13 percent worry "not at all."
- Fifty-two percent of those surveyed believe that protection of the environment should be given priority, even at the risk of curbing economic growth, while 37 percent believe that economic growth should be given priority, even if the environment suffers to some extent. Six percent felt environmental protection and economic growth should be valued equally.

- Forty-nine percent believe that the Arctic National Wildlife Refuge in Alaska should be opened up for oil exploration, and 47 percent oppose exploration.
- Twenty-five percent of people surveyed believe the quality of the environment in the United States is "getting better," while 67 percent believe that it is "getting worse."

According to a Harris Poll taken in August 2005:

- Forty-seven percent of those surveyed believe the government's involvement in protecting the environment is "too little," 32 percent believe that the government's involvement in environmental protection is "about right," and 19 percent believe the government's involvement is "too much."
- Sixty-three percent believe that the general public has done "less than their share" to help solve environmental problems," 10 percent believe the general public has done "more than their share," and 26 percent believe that the general public's contribution has been "about right."
- Seventy-four percent agree that "protecting the environment is so important that requirements and standards cannot be too high, and continuing environmental improvements must be made regardless of cost." Twenty-four percent disagreed.

Glossary

biodiversity: The variation of life forms in a particular location or **ecosystem**. Generally, an ecosystem is considered to be in better health if it has a wider variety of plants and animals, and a species is considered to be healthier if a wider range of subspecies exist. Also called "biological diversity."

biosphere: The outer shell of the earth—encompassing its land, air, and water—inhabited by living creatures.

concession: An area of land that is set aside for the protection of particular plants or animals. People who live or farm in a concession are compensated by their government for living and working in ways that protect threatened species. Also called a "conservation concession."

conservation: The protection of wild plants and animals, as well as the protection of their natural **habitats**.

ecosystem: Any designated portion of the **biosphere** under study or consideration. The term *ecosystem* derives from the words *ecology* and *system*, and refers to the idea that an area's plants, animals, other life forms, soil, and water exist together and rely on each other.

endangered species: A species of animal, plant, or lower life form that is in danger of becoming extinct. Species are considered endangered when their population numbers reach very low levels, or when their **habitat** is rapidly disappearing.

fauna: Animal life.

fishery: A region where fishing for a particular type of fish is concentrated, because the fish exist there in large numbers.

flora: Plant life.

global warming: The gradual warming of the earth's atmosphere, caused largely by human activities, including the burning of fossil fuels. Also called "global climate change."

habitat: The place where a particular species lives and thrives. Many species face the risk of extinction because their habitats (wetlands, rainforests, or open range, for example) become smaller as human development consumes more land.

indigenous: A term that refers to people, other life forms, or objects that originate in a particular place. "Indigenous people" means people who are "native" to a certain area, or whose ancestors have always lived in an area, as opposed to more recent "settlers" or "immigrants."

migration: The act of moving from one place to another to find food or habitat. Certain North American birds, for example, undergo an annual migration, flying south to find food during the winter and returning to the north to nest and raise young during the spring and fall.

poaching: Illegal hunting or fishing, particularly of a species that is protected because it is threatened or endangered.

threatened species: A species of animal, plant, or lower life form, that risks becoming extinct, but that is in less danger than so-called **endangered species**.

wildlife refuge: An area where plants or animals are protected, usually by a government. Within a wildlife refuge, animals typically cannot be hunted, and they do not share habitat with their natural prey.

Organizations to Contact

The editors have compiled the following list of organizations concerned with the issues debated in this book. The descriptions are derived from materials provided by the organizations. All have publications or information available for interested readers. The list was compiled on the date of publication of the present volume; the information provided here may change. Be aware that many organizations take several weeks or longer to respond to inquiries, so allow as much time as possible.

Arctic Power
PO Box 100220
Anchorage, AK 99510
(907) 274-2697
e-mail: mail@anwr.org
Web site: www.anwr.org
Arctic Power, based in Anchorage, Alaska, is a grassroots, nonprofit citizen's organization founded in April 1992. Its ten thousand members work to encourage congressional and presidential approval of oil exploration and production within the Coastal Plain of the Arctic National Wildlife Refuge. Its Web site includes photos, fact sheets, and multimedia presentations, and a report titled *Making the Case for ANWR Development.*

Center for Global Food Issues (CGFI)
PO Box 202
Churchville, VA 24421
(540) 337-6354
fax: (540) 337-8593
e-mail: cgfi@hughes.net
Web site: www.cgfi.org
The Center for Global Food Issues (CGFI) researches and analyzes food issues and their connections to the environment, and educates

farmers and others about the effects of food policies and farming practices on the environment. CGFI believes that environmental conservation can be achieved through wise practices of free and global trade. The organization publishes the *Global Food Quarterly*, as well as speeches and a blog available through its Web site. Recent reports include *Rachel Carson Syndrome: Jumping to Pesticide Conclusions in the Global Frog Crisis*.

Competitive Enterprise Institute (CEI)
1001 Connecticut Avenue NW, Suite 1250
Washington, DC 20036
(202) 331-1010
fax: (202) 331-0640
e-mail: info@cei.org
Web site: www.cei.org
The Competitive Enterprise Institute (CEI), founded in 1984, is a nonprofit public policy organization dedicated to advancing the principles of free enterprise and limited government. CEI argues that the best solutions to environmental problems come from individuals making their own choices in a free marketplace. It publishes opinion and analysis pieces on its online *EnviroWire* and an online *Daily Update*.

Defenders of Wildlife
1130 17th Street NW
Washington, DC 20036
(800) 385-9712
e-mail: defenders@mail.defenders.org
Web site: www.defenders.org
Defenders of Wildlife is a group of scientists, attorneys, and educators dedicated to the protection of all native wild animals and plants in their natural communities. Using education, legal action, and scientific research, the organization focuses on species conservation, habitat conservation, and policy leadership. Defenders of Wildlife publishes a magazine, *Defenders*, as well as print and electronic newsletters.

Greenpeace
702 H Street NW
Washington, DC 20001
(800) 326-0959
(202) 462-1177
e-mail: info@wdc.greenpeace.org
Web site: www.greenpeace.org
Greenpeace is an international nonprofit organization which accepts no funding from governments or corporations. Founded in 1971, it focuses on worldwide threats to the planet's biodiversity and environment, and directs attention to its mission through public acts of nonviolent civil disobedience. Greenpeace publishes news releases and technical reports, including *America's Keystone Forests: Mapping the Next 100 Years of Forest Protection* and *Rethinking Sustainability: A New Paradigm for Fisheries Management.*

National Resources Defense Council (NRDC)
40 West 20th Street
New York, NY 10011
(212) 727-2700
fax: (212) 727-1773
e-mail: nrdcinfo@nrdc.org
Web site: www.nrdc.org
National Resources Defense Council (NRDC), one of the most powerful environmental groups in the United States, works to support pro-environmental legislation and defeat anti-environment legislation. Specifically, it calls on government to work with its citizens to protect endangered species, reduce pollution, and create a sustainable way of life for humankind. NRDC publishes a quarterly magazine, *OnEarth*, and e-mail bulletins including *Earth Action*, *Legislative Watch*, and *This Green Life*.

Property and Environmental Research Center (PERC)
2048 Analysis Drive, Suite A
Bozeman, MT 59718
(406) 587-9591
e-mail: perc@perc.org
Web site: www.perc.org
The originator of the approach known as free market environmentalism, the Property and Environment Research Center (PERC) is the nation's oldest and largest institute dedicated to original research on ways to harness market forces to encourage resource stewardship and environmental quality. The group addresses such issues as the Endangered Species Act, environmental education, and environmental federalism. Publications include a newsletter for students, *Environmental Examiner*; a series of lesson plans that can be downloaded in pdf format; and articles including "Saving Fisheries with Free Markets."

U.S. Fish and Wildlife Service
1849 C Street NW
Washington, DC 20240
(800) 344-WILD
Web site: www.fws.gov
The U.S. Fish and Wildlife Service was created by Congress in 1871 to help stop the dramatic decline of several species during the late 19th century. Its mission is "working with others to conserve, protect and enhance fish, wildlife, and plants and their habitats for the continuing benefit of the American people." The agency publishes a magazine, the *Fish & Wildlife News*, and through its Web site offers reports, news releases, videos, and live Web cams.

The World Conservation Union (IUCN)
Rue Mauverney 28
Gland
1196
Switzerland
41 (22) 999-0000
fax: 41 (22) 999-0002
e-mail: webmaster@ iucn.org
Web site: www.iucn.org
The World Conservation Union (IUCN), less commonly called the International Union for Conservation of Nature and Natural Resources, was founded in 1948 after an international conference held in France. Its members, including ten thousand scientists and other experts from 181 countries, work to connect scientific understanding of conservation issues with official policy, by bringing scientists and representatives together in dialogue. The group issues an annual "Red List" of threatened and endangered species worldwide. The IUCN Web site features books, articles, news releases, and fact sheets.

World Wildlife Fund (WWF)
1250 Twenty-Fourth Street NW
PO Box 97180
Washington, DC 20090
(202) 293-4800
Web site: www.worldwildlife.org
The World Wildlife Fund (WWF), established in 1961, works in one hundred countries around the world to protect natural areas and wild animals and plants, including endangered species. With almost 5 million members, it is the largest conservation organization in the world. WWF issues periodic press releases about its work, and publishes an e-mail newsletter. News releases, photos, free e-cards, and action alerts are available from its Web site.

For Further Reading

Books

Rick Bass, *Caribou Rising: Defending the Porcupine Herd, Gwich'in Culture, and the Arctic National Wildlife Refuge*. San Francisco: Sierra Club Books, 2004. Bass, a nature writer as well as an avid hunter and a former oil and gas geologist, recounts his extended stay with the Gwich-'in people of northern Alaska and argues that preserving their ancient culture is more worthy than drilling for oil.

Tom Bethell, *The Politically Incorrect Guide to Science*. Washington, DC: Regnery, 2005. An entertaining and readable analysis of how political motivations influence so-called scientific conclusions on issues including extinction, global warming, and evolution.

Adrian Dorst, *Rainforest America: The Beautiful and Endangered Pacific Rainforest from Northern California to Alaska*. Toronto: Warwick, 2007. Dorst, an award-winning Canadian photographer, explores the two-thousand-mile-long Pacific rainforest and the plants and animals that inhabit it.

Paul Driessen, *Eco-Imperialism: Green Power. Black Death*. Bellevue, WA: Merril Press, 2003. Driessen argues that radical environmentalism, in its pursuit of sustainability, harms economic development in poor countries, leading to millions of unnecessary deaths.

Sharon Guyup, ed., *State of the Wild: A Global Portrait of Wildlife, Wildlands, and Oceans*. Washington, DC: Island Press, 2005. An anthology of essays by leading conservationists, with analysis of news highlights and statistics dealing with a variety of conservation issues.

Christopher C. Horner, *The Politically Incorrect Guide to Global Warming (and Environmentalism)*. Washington, DC: Regnery, 2007. An entertaining analysis of how environmentalists manipulate scientific data for political gain.

Tora Johnson, *Entanglements: The Intertwined Fates of Whales and Fishermen*. Gainesville: University Press of Florida, 2005. In this volume the author, an ecology professor and former commercial fisherman, examines how commercial fishermen can best avoid accidentally entangling endangered whales.

John Charles Kunich, *Killing Our Oceans: Dealing with the Mass Extinction of Marine Life*. Westport, CT: Praeger, 2006. An overview of basic oceanography and an exploration of how human actions are destroying the oceans.

Richard Mackay, *The Atlas of Endangered Species*. London: Earthscan, 2005. This revision of a 2001 atlas includes maps showing habitats and distribution of various species, human effects, and the effects of global climate change.

Thomas Marent, *Rainforest*. New York: Dorling Kindersley, 2006. More than five hundred beautiful photographs of plants and animals, taken by Marent, a Swiss photographer, who has visited rainforests around the world over a period of more than sixteen years.

John Nielson, *Condor: To the Brink and Back—The Life and Times of One Giant Bird*. New York: HarperCollins, 2006. An account of the California condor's near-extinction and efforts to rescue it by capturing the few remaining birds and raising them in zoos.

David Owen and David Pemberton, *Tasmanian Devil: A Unique and Threatened Animal*. New South Wales, Australia: Allen & Unwin, 2005. A natural history of a little-understood creature that is facing extinction due to a rapidly spreading form of cancer.

Ruth Padel, *Tigers in Red Weather: A Quest for the Last Wild Tigers*. New York: Walker, 2006. A multilayered memoir of Padel's travels to see tigers in the wild and her conversations with scientists and conservationists about the social and economic complexities of the issues surrounding tiger extinction.

Brian Payton, *Shadow of the Bear: Travels in the Vanishing Wilderness*. Toronto: Viking Canada, 2006. Payton chronicles eight trips he took to observe bears in different parts of the world—including the American brown bear of the Colorado plateau—and examines the importance of bears in art, literature, and the economy.

Doug Peacock and Andrea Peacock, *The Essential Grizzly: The Mingled Fates of Men and Bears*. Guilford, CT: Lyons Press, 2006. The authors argue that grizzly bears must be saved from extinction, even though human contact with grizzlies cannot be made without danger.

Norbert Rosing, *The World of the Polar Bear*. Richmond Hill, Ontario, Canada: Firefly, 2006. A collection of images of polar bears and their habitat taken by Rosing, a German photographer.

Howard Smith, *In the Company of Wild Bears: A Celebration of Backcountry Grizzlies and Black Bears,*. Guilford, CT: Lyons Press, 2006. Lavishly illustrated with photographs by Michael H. Francis, this volume combines Smith's own observances of bears in the wild across the United States with informational sidebars about how to view bears in the wild safely and sensitively.

Malcolm Tait, ed., *Going, Going, Gone? Animals and Plants on the Brink of Extinction and How You Can Help.* London: Think Publishing, 2006. Edited by naturalist Tait, this book examines one hundred species under threat, each nominated by a different conservation organization from around the world. Each species is beautifully photographed and contact information for each organization is included.

Jonathan Waterman, *Where Mountains Are Nameless: Passion and Politics in the Arctic National Wildlife Refuge.* New York: Norton, 2005. A collection of essays detailing the author's observations over twenty years of travel through the Arctic National Wildlife Refuge, and including a brief biography of conservationists Olaus and Mardy Murie, who helped establish the refuge.

Periodicals

Marc Alexander, "Last of the Cuban Crocodile?" *Americas*, January–February 2006.

Jennifer C. Berkshire, "I Won't Take the Cod, Thank You," *Christian Science Monitor*, December 15, 2006.

Andrew Buncombe and Severin Carrell, "Melting Planet," *Independent* (London), October 2, 2005.

Barrie Clement, "Hippopotamus Among 26,000 New Species on Endangered List," *Independent* (UK), May 1, 2006.

Steve Connor, "Earth Faces 'Catastrophic Loss of Species,'" *Independent* (UK), July 20, 2006.

Sarah DeWeerdt, "Extinction: Bye, Bye, Birdie," *World Watch*, December 15, 2006.

Daniel Duane, "Sacrificial Ram," *Mother Jones*, March–April 2005.

Daniel Glick, "Back from the Brink," *Smithsonian*, September 2005.

Bob Holmes, "Bag a Trophy, Save a Species," *NewScientist Environment*, January 6, 2007. http://environment.newscientist.com.

Jane Kay, "Where Are All the Birds?" *San Francisco Chronicle*, July 4, 2006.

Keith Kloor, "Sagebrush Showdown," *Audubon*, January–February 2007.

Winona La Duke, "Saving the Seri Sea Turtles," *AlterNet*, December 15, 2006. www.alternet.org.

Forrest Laws, "Farmers Will Protect Endangered Species," *Western Farm Press*, July 28, 2005.

Sharon Levy, "The Little Mouse That Got in the Way," *OnEarth*, Winter 2007.

Ben Lieberman, "Alaska Oil Drilling Myths," *Washington Times*, December 20, 2005.

Amanda Griscom Little, "Endangered Species Act Gets Toxic Tune-Up," *AlterNet*, October 11, 2005. www.alternet.org.

Robert McClure, "Your Favorite Seafood May Be in Peril, Study Says," *Seattle Post-Intelligencer*, November 3, 2006.

Robert McClure and Lisa Stiffler, "Flaws in Habitat Conservation Plans Threaten Scores of Species," *Seattle Post-Intelligencer*, May 3, 2005.

Bryn Nelson, "Unhappy End to Fish Story," *Newsday*, November 3, 2006.

James Owen, "Amazon Logging Twice as Heavy as Thought, Images Show," *National Geographic News*, October 20, 2005.

"Polar Bear Politics," *Wall Street Journal*, January 3, 2007.

Jeremy Rifkin, "The Risks of Too Much City," *Washington Post*, December 18, 2006.

Will Rizzo, "Return of the Jaguar?" *Smithsonian*, December 2005.

"A Roaring Return for Grizzlies," *Weekly Reader*, senior ed., January 27, 2006.

Roxana Robinson, "Watching as the World Vanishes," *Boston Globe*, January 1, 2006.

Seattle Post-Intelligencer Editorial Board, "Endangered Species: A Law That Works," *Seattle Post-Intelligencer*, September 11, 2005.

Jeff Shaw, "Marines and Manatees," *E: The Environmental Magazine*, January–February 2005.

Brian Skoloff, "Florida Panthers Threatened as Development Overtakes Habitat," *America's Intelligence Wire*, December 4, 2006.

Tiffany Trent, "Midas's Turtle," *Orion*, May–June 2005.

Ted Williams, "Law of Salvation," *Audubon*, November–December 2005.

———, "Something's Fishy," *Audubon*, May–June 2005.

Kurt Williamsen, "Destruction of the Oyster Industry," *New American*, June 26, 2006.

Web Sites

The Commons: Environmental Alarmism Archives (http://commons blog.org/archives/cat_environmental_alarmism.php). A collection of blog postings and other readings analyzing the harmful effects of exaggerating the seriousness of environmental problems, including endangered species.

Eco.Imperialism (www.eco-imperialism.com/main.php). A collection of writings by site founder Paul Driessen and others exploring the ways the environmental movement slows economic development and harms humans in the process.

Environmental Literacy Council (www.enviroliteracy.org/index. php). An educational site geared toward teachers of students in kindergarten through twelfth grade.

Grist Magazine (www.grist.org). An online magazine featuring independent environmental news and commentary. Offers a free e-mail newsletter.

Worldwatch Institute (www.worldwatch.org). Offering "independent research for an environmentally sustainable and socially just society," the site features surveys, articles, news releases, and other publications.

Index

Picture Credits